Doktrina Kristiana

Doktrina Kristiana

Art Saguinsin and Artusard Renault

Published by Artusard Renault, 2025.

DOKTRINA KRISTIANA

First edition. August 8, 2025.

ISBN: 979-8231867998

Written by Art Saguinsin and Artusard Renault.

Artusard Renault

TABLE OF CONTENTS

Preface

The book, " Doktrina Kristiana (Doctrine of Christianity) ' is the revelation of the great mystery which the Holy Bible has unveiled to the people in these last days. A must read, learn as it is founded by the mystery of the Word that has been sealed for generations until revealed for understanding and obedience by the appointed people of this last generation, who obey its principles for salvation. Reading the content of this book may be a realization of the knowledge towards salvation and a lamp to those individuals who thirst for truth about spiritual knowledge about salvation. There are a lot of amazing things one can realize from this book, regardless of political and religious ideology as it is good and intended to be known and used by all races of men on earth.

This book and its contents must not be mistaken with the early book that contained the Catholic Creed," Doctrina Christiana", which was one of the first printed books written by Fray Juan de Plasencia in Manila, Philippines. On June 20, 1593, Governor Gomez Perez Dasmarinas wrote a letter to King Philip II of Spain conveying his concerns for the need to print the book and likewise, seeking the latter's advice on the pricing method of the book that was printed in Spanish and Tagalog.

Introduction

The main objective of this book is to impart and propagate the Law and Doctrine of the Christ to all the inhabitants of the earth. The law of the Christ nowadays, is different from the Mosaic law, (Judaism), because the law of the Christ is not only ten but, more than ten and there are laws in the Ten Commandments that had been amended during the time of Jesus. If the Ten Commandments were strictly observed and obeyed during that time, much more during the Christian dispensation where there are more commandments of the Christ. The law and doctrine of the Christ are discussed and explained as you read them.

Why have I chosen to write about the philosophy of Christian doctrine? Since this is a confession of acquired Christian faith founded on the Word in the bible that has ripened into a firm belief , this should be pronounced and propagated to the Christian world and all the inhabitants of the world to embrace. We should realize that physical death is just temporal, for we shall all rise at the appointed time after death. And our next destiny is to face and account ourselves in the presence of our Creator in the day of judgment.

Therefore, while we are here on earth we should realize that there are things we need to know in order to be prepared spiritually when that day comes. I believe that by this piece of work I would be able to impart spiritual insight to all, the spiritual knowledge they should keep in their minds and hearts that will serve as the key to their salvation.

I go spiritual this time. With my spiritual interest and passion to learn about spiritual things, I began to search the truth about life after death. For several years, I have studied and read many inspirational and spiritual writings of prophets and apostles in the bible as I believe that the bible, being the Word of God is indubitably the only source of spiritual truths , knowledge and wisdom.

For many years of my profound research and quest about the Christian doctrine from various congregational doctrines, I have learned many things and ultimately contained with this piece of work. I won't say that this is the ultimate belief you should embrace, but as Truth-Seeker, we have the free will to choose. I am just presenting this as guide and knowledge that is founded on the Word in the bible and no personal pronouncement contained herein compels you to embrace this belief, but everything lies on your very own personal decision.

The very instruction of the bible in 1John 4:1, which says, " Test every spirit if it is of God" meaning we should test the teachings of that preacher or teacher whether it is right or wrong. Therefore, by using logical thinking we will be able to discern whether it is correct or not.

Logic, therefore is very crucial before we approve the assertions of a church leader because what is at stake here is the salvation of our soul in the days to come. It is where our salvation lies, so we must make sure that logical thinking works in order for us to be saved, thus, the bible instructs everyone to be wise nowadays, because *many false prophets preaching and promising salvation are out of this world.*

To prophesy is to preach. Philosophy is defined as an attitude, viewpoint, thinking, idea, value, beliefs and way of life while Logic is the science of sound reasoning, judgment, common sense. If we combine philosophy with logic the outcome is correct results of our thinking and reasoning. Logic gives correct judgment and reasoning as it leads us to the right path. Therefore, logic is necessary in our decision. With the use of common thinking and right sensing, we can think logically, therefore, we are able to discern what is right and what is wrong.

CHAPTER 1

The Holy Bible- The Foundation of Salvation and Truth

The Holy Bible is a book that contains the Word of God which was written by His chosen people, particularly the prophets and disciples in the Old and New Testaments. . The Holy bible constitutes two parts: The Old Testament and The New Testament. The Old Testament which is the first part contains 39 books while the New Testament contains 27 books. This makes a total of 66 books in the bible and written by more than 40 people of God. Where must we derive the basis for our salvation, but the holy bible and not from men's own conceived ideas and ideology. Never say that we have become bookies when we base our assertions from the bible because it is the only source of the truths and no other book. But, if we say that when a church leader is no bookies in his preaching, then begin asking yourselves where he got his assertions and pronouncements.

Remember, salvation is no joke and that truth must never be distorted, otherwise, the bible instructs us to curse those who distort, change and add anything in the word (thus, the bible says) So, watch out those professing prophets, God's messenger or those who claim that they are sent to teach, when in fact, he is fooling around. Your material and spiritual losses are at hand. You can be bookies when the source and foundation of your allegations are derived from man's intellectual creations, but setting aside the bible.

Origin of the Holy Bible.

Who wrote the Holy Bible?

How did the bible become the basis for man's salvation? Is this written by ordinary men? Many people who do not believe in the bible would skeptically say, it was just written and conceived by ordinary men. We can say that everything on earth was created by God while He gave us the power to produce things out of our own effort to survive and live according to what we can afford. Man manufactures many things for our own benefit in order that life may continue and progress. You can just imagine that everything we eat, wear, and read is made by the hands of men, and conclusively, the bible was written by men.

Speaking of the bible as the focal point of the issue, we may think how it came to being. How was it assembled and made into an organized book ? How does it differ from all other books? All we know is that, it is a compilation of the Word of God containing the books of Genesis which tells about the beginning and creation of everything up to Revelation which tells us about the end of the whole story. Let us refer one of the verses which tells us who wrote this book. In *II Peter 1:20-24*, reads," *Knowing this first, that no prophecy of the Scripture is of any private interpretation*". In other words, the verse tells us that it cannot be written by just an ordinary man. This proves that the bible did not come from men's conceived story or imagination , because according to the verse, it cannot emanate from man's private interpretation nor from his own will, but from the holy men of God who spoke as they were moved by the Holy Ghost. The Word came from God who spoke to men.

Where else do you think the bible would emanate ? Who do you think would write it? Definitely, it is not the animals who would write it because if chicken, would write it, it cannot be read by humans, it would be scratched and mutilated instead. If you believe God gave it to men to write, definitely, He would give it to men to write in order to be read and understood by human beings. Otherwise, if the bible was not written by men what would be the basis of our salvation and our future .If we shall read everything from the bible, this will contain words that man could never think nor conceive in their minds. This consists of words of prophecy , words of exhortations and as a whole the laws of God. If men could think of his own ideas to write and say, certain verse in *Proverbs 16:9* proves that men think of his own course. We can notice from the bible that ordinary men could not think such phrases and wisdom that are written in the bible. It is said that men by nature are sinners, therefore, men would not dare to write about holiness nor heavenly ideas, except the holy men of God. Just think that these were given by God to the chosen people, to be taught and spoken of, and finally to serve as the basis of our salvation.

What do you think would be the foundation of men's source of knowledge about salvation? Will you just believe and entrust your soul to some few men whom you do not know? Where did they get their teachings about salvation? The book of II Peter 3:15 reads, "*And account that the long suffering of our Lord is salvation; even as our beloved brother Paul also according to the wisdom given unto him hath written unto you.*" The verse tells us that the Word of instructions is only given to the chosen ones who have the Holy Ghost, and not to just an ordinary men The chosen men were moved by the Holy Spirit of God to write the bible. As it is written in I Chronicles 28:9. which reads, " *And thou Solomon, my son, know thou the God of the father, and serve him with a perfect heart and with a willing mind for the Lord searcheth all hearts, and understandeth all the imaginations of the thoughts ; if thou forsake him he will cast thee off forever.*" This verse proves that men who wrote the bible were chosen by God because they could not write and prophesy without the leading of the Holy Spirit. The holy men of God would not be able to write the bible if they were not tested, while their hearts were searched by the Holy Spirit sent by God. It doesn't mean they did not commit sin. They did, but God chose them and had plans for them even before they were conceived in their mothers' wombs. They feared God as they obeyed His commandments. In the same manner that Scriptures provide us wisdom and knowledge toward righteousness. II Timothy 3:16 reads, " *All Scriptures is given by inspiration of God, and is profitable for doctrine, for reproof, for correction, for instruction in righteousness."*

The verse mentioned will attest to the truth that the written Word will provide us knowledge about salvation and make men wise. Let us read another basis to make the testimony concrete, which tells that our knowledge of salvation through Jesus Christ will save us. *II Timothy 3:15* reads" *and that from a child thou hast known the Holy Scriptures which are able to make thee wise unto salvation through faith which is in Christ Jesus."* So, if anyone wants wisdom and knowledge, he or she may ask God for it by means of prayers. This is attested in the book of James 1:5 *which reads," If any of you lack wisdom, let him ask of God. That giveth to all men liberally, and upbraideth not; and it shall be given him"*

Guarantee That The Bible Is The Authentic Word Of God

Let us read Proverbs 8:8, " *All the words of my mouth are in righteousness, there is nothing forward or perverse in them*". God Himself is the one confirming that His Word is Righteousness. There is nothing forward and perverse in them. There is no doubt that everything written in the bible is authentic as attested by the said verse that is clearly written and answered the question. What are some knowledge that man never knew until revealed by the bible? Another proof that the bible is the original and authentic Word of God is the mystery of men's innocence about the facts that have happened or are happening on earth which the bible reveals and have been known to men. Like for example, in the past people believed that the earth was flat, however, an astronomer named Galileo Galeli found out that it is round. Galileo revealed his findings and made him one of the controversial figures in the Italian history. Another one is the disputable theory of Charles Darwin of the evolution of life in which it was stated that men transformed from the so-called Apemen. The Java men and Cro- Magno men transferred to natural men,accordingly. It was believed that the so-called Apemen were believed to be the transformatory origin of natural men.

Logically, if Darwin really asserted this theory and belief , that would be a disputable issue nowadays, because if man transformed from the ape to Java man then to Cro Magno man, and gradually to natural man, then it would happen the same thing all over again that man would transform again from gorillas or apes nowadays. It may become a continuous life cycle, because according to theory it is the evolution and origin of man. In the 20th century, the first men made a historic landing on the moon. They took photographs of the earth while on the space capsule. It showed the beautifully-rounded figure of the earth. Would you believe that had it not for the first men on the moon who took photos of ;the earth, it would not really be proven that the earth is really round just in the 20th century?

This fact is already proven and told in the bible thousands of years ago which came ahead of modern technology of modern men. The prophet Isaiah attested the fact in Isaiah 40:22, " *It is that sitteth upon the circle of the earth, and the inhabitants thereof are as grasshoppers that stretcheth out the heavens as curtain, and spreadeth them to put as a tent to dwell in* . This assertion of the prophet Isaiah proves that thousands of years ago, the earth was confirmed to be round (circle as stated in the verse) in which the succeeding generations had never known until the 20th century. This became a dispute for many generations by scientists and philosophers and mathematicians as well in olden times. These stated facts confirm also that the bible is also a scientific book.

The Discovery of Scrolls

Two thousand years ago, the first Apostles wrote the teachings of Jesus Christ in the animal skin or the so-called scrolls. Apostle Paul, who has the most number of writings in the bible traveled Asia Minor and preached the gospel of salvation to the people. The scrolls were preserved and kept by the church-people from generation to generation and were eventually found by the Jewish group in Israel called *Essense*. They took care of it until , finally handed to the bible scholars, who translated the Hebrew writings into Greek and eventually into English language. In the 17th century England, scholars translated the bible into English version by a certain priest named William Tyndale. During those days there was a great persecution among the true believers and disciples of the Christ. The reigning King at that time ordered the burning of bibles and other Christian paraphernalia. The tyranny of the ruling king prohibited the readings of the gospel and gatherings among Christians. The defiant, who would disobey the order would be branded as heretics. They would be prosecuted in the Inquisition and if found guilty of violating the law, they would be mercilessly burned to death alive.

Inquisition was the court of trial by the Inquisitors in the Dark Age Europe.

In the 19th century Palestine, a shepherd boy while on his way to the farm near the Dead Sea, discovered earthen jars in a cave. He found out that these jars contained scrolls with Aramaic writings in it. These pieces of scrolls were later brought to Italy for analysis by the bible scholars. Scholars concluded that writings in the scrolls could be part of those writings by the Apostles during the time of Jesus Christ.

CHAPTER 2

The True Teachings of the Christ

As events occur around the world , there are phenomena that foretell to be the signs of times. We should be aware that some events that occur are foretold in the bible. There will be confusion and deception when it comes to current events now. It is realistic that misinformation creates commotion. How can we identify the true messenger of God nowadays? Are today's evangelists, preachers and teachers telling the truth of the gospel? When the teacher of truth teaches the Word that no other teachers can defy, nor can it be denied based from the facts in the bible, then he is telling the truth. Justify and test him by the way he lives , if it is in adherence to what the bible is teaching about the true teacher of faith. Not all of them is telling the truth, by reason that they have different motives and interests.

The bible tells that not all who calls on the Lord will be saved, but only those who do the will of the Father. Not all will be saved in the last day, but many of them will say that they drove out evils in the Name of the Lord, but the Lord will said unto them, " Away from me evil doers, I do not know you!"

Why were they driven away by the Lord? It is because these people could have done evil in the performance of preaching the Word in perverse manner while the Lord searched their hearts and found to be wicked. They do and teach things that are not founded in the bible and do not conform with the teachings of the Christ. Many false prophets are doing it in this world nowadays. Try to find the true teachings of the Christ in order not to be misled by these deceivers. In II Corinthians 13:5 says, " *Examine yourselves to see whether you are in the faith; test yourselves. Do you not realize that Christ Jesus is in you, unless of course, you fail the test? And I trust that you will discover that we have not failed the test.*" Many self-professed believers believe that they are still in the Christ and yet, doing what is against the will of the Lord. The verse is telling us to examine and test yourselves, if you are still following the teachings of the Christ. You can't say that you are already saved even in the judgment day because you are already a Christian and have accepted the Christ as your personal Lord and Savior. No, it doesn't count because how will you be saved if you have been doing wrong and keeping yourselves away from the teachings of Christ? No way to be saved. Test yourselves if you are still in the right track of the instructions of the gospel, otherwise, the Christ will deny you in the last day.

In some events, some religious groups are indoctrinating their beliefs. People should feel free to watch and hear their teachings in order to determine if it is from God as the instruction says, in I John 4:1 says, " *Beloved, believe not every spirit, but try the spirits whether they are of God; because many false prophets are gone out into the world." It is not bad to compare one teaching from another teachings in order to test the doctrine of the teachings and thereby giving way for the truth to come out.* This is instructed to us in *Ecclesiastes 7:27* " *Behold, this have I found, saith the Preacher, <u>counting one by one, to find out the account;</u>"* It may be normal that one may say that he or she is already a Christian and spiritually saved, as what some modern day Christians are claiming. They claim it that way after receiving their conversion from their respective churches in professing their Christian faith. Some may still be babes in faith being fed with milk or the basic teachings and some have been eating meat or having been elders in the Word. It may not be easy if one who receives a new faith in the Christ would say that he is already saved when he has to pass through the process of being a Christian. You will pass the test of fire as in gold that is being polished to see it's authenticity. There are lots of tests to pass by that should be overcome while you keep embracing the faith you received.

One may even say, he is saved until the last day. It is wrong to have that notion because being a Christian is a long process while on earth. One will pass through an eye of a needle before he can say, he is already saved in the last day. One should finish the race like Paul, who said with assurance that he had finished the race. That was said by Paul when he was already old enough and had finished the propagation of the gospel. He said that phrase because he knew he was nearing his death. The apostle Paul went into a rigid process of being a disciple of the Christ which in the end had made it. He was the only apostle who had a great task of performing the work of a disciple and to him, the mysteries were revealed that were not revealed to other apostles. His long and adventurous journey in propagating the gospel was full of struggle that he even imperiled his life in many instances. He fought his enemies, but not in the flesh but in the spirit in order to win them and reveal the mystery of the gospel. The book of the Ephesians 6:12-17 say, "

For we wrestle not against the flesh and blood, but against principalities, against power, against the ruler of the darkness of this world, against spiritual wickedness in high places, wherefore take unto you the whole armor of God, that ye may be able to withstand in the evil day, and having done all, stand having your loins girt about the truth, having on the breastplate of righteousness, and your feet shod with the preparation of the gospel of peace, above all, taking the shield of faith, wherewith ye shall be able to quench all the fiery darts of the wicked. And take the helmet of salvation, and the sword of the Spirit, which is the sword of God."

This was how the apostle Paul shielded and protected himself in all his undertakings before he went to confront the spiritual enemies of the Lord in spreading the gospel of Christ in the enemy's jurisdiction.

Serving and Worshipping God

Church goers normally go to church to worship their Gods and have fellowship with brethren. In fact, people have other gods to worship. They have different ways of worshipping them, however, there are other ways of serving and worshipping the true living God. Remember that God is a spirit; and they that worship him must worship Him in spirit and in truth (John 4:34). When we worship Him in spirit, we have to present ourselves with clean spirit, meaning we should have asked forgiveness from our transgressions. God searches our heart and he knows whether we are sincere and repentant from our shortcomings . In that manner we serve Him in spirit. On the other hand, in physical world, we serve God by doing good as we lead a clean life that is pleasing to Him. We sing praises and hymns and utter phrases with thanksgiving. We submit ourselves to His will while we keep ourselves away from lusts and sins of this world. *Romans 6:12 says, "Let us not sin therefore reign in your mortal body, that ye should obey it in the lusts thereof."* Submitting the parts of our body for righteousness to perform acts that may produce good results and benefit others is an act of worship and serving God. By serving and helping others in times of need is an act of worship and service. If you work for others such as your employer, an individual who has contracted you; your elders; authority or anybody else that you have dealings in good faith with and you perform acts sincerely, then you are already serving and worshipping God. *Romans 6:13 says, "Neither yield ye your members as instruments of unrighteousness unto sin; but yield yourselves unto God, as those that are alive from the dead, and your members as instruments of righteousness unto God."*

Extending and giving alms to poor and needy , especially those who are victims of nature's fury that are in dire need of material necessities in times of crisis are ways of serving God. *The bible says, in Proverbs 19:17 says, "He that hath pity upon the poor lendeth unto the LORD; and that which he hath given will he pay him again."*

Obedience to the Will of God

Believers are obedient and respecter of men's laws. They submit to authority because governing authority will not be installed and inducted for men to obey if it is not the will of God. If you believe that God is in control of situations even if you hate the authority, you are compelled to obey because their emergence to power will not be possible had it not for the will of the Supreme authority, that is God. What does the bible say about the inducted authority in the government of men? Let us read I Peter 2:17 "*Honor all but as the servants of God. Honor all men, love the brothers and Fear God. Honor the king.*"In 1Peter 2: 13-14 read, " *Submit yourselves to every ordinance of man for the Lord's sake. Whether it be to the king as supreme, or unto governor as unto them that are sent by him for the punishment of evildoers and for the praise of them that do well.*"For the sake of Christ believers obey whatever situations arise because God knows who deserve to rule and who deserve to be removed in power in its right time.

As believers submit to the law of man, the former should politely and respectfully render what is due others. If others are honored because of their accomplishments and achievements, believers should also honor them and respect them as what the book of

Romans 13:7 says, " *Render therefore to all their dues; tribute to who tribute is due; custom to whom wisdom ; fear to whom fear; honor to whom honor.*" Again for the sake of Christ we give what is due them, respect and honor as commanded. While Christian believers are inevitably mingling with unbelievers with wisdom, the former shall also believe in the manner that is in conformity with church's laws. Let us read Matthew 10:16," *Behold, I send you forth as sheep in the midst of wolves, be ye therefore, wise as serpents, and harmless as doves.*"

Believers would not cause unbelievers any trouble, but rather would treat others gently, wise and harmless. It is also an instruction to the believers to love their enemies despite indifferences in beliefs and doctrines. For genuine Christians, the fruits of the Holy Spirit are manifested and served as light to unbelievers. Matthew 5:42-44 read, "Give to him that asketh thee, and from him that would borrow of thee turn not thou away. Ye have heard that it hath been said, Thou shalt love thy neighbor, and hate thine enemy. But I say unto you. Love your enemies, bless them that curse you. Do good to them which despitefully use you, and persecute you." The bible affirms also that you, as Christians are the light of the world.

The True Religion and its Meaning

What is a True Religion? What is meant by Religion? Let us read James 1:27, " Pure religion and undefiled before God and the Fathers is this, To visit the fatherless and widows in their affliction, and to keep himself unspotted from the world." Religion comes from the Greek words, "re", meaning again, "lego", meaning "tie", so if the two words are combined this will mean, " to tie again". Where should we be tied again? Of course, to the teachings or laws of God in order to be saved. Other forms of religions on earth believe that life does not end after dying, for example the Hindu believes that after they die their soul will transfer to another form of being or creation like animals, trees and other things around us, while others teach their followers that they will go to a place like paradise and that hell is just on earth. Other's beliefs say that there is no heaven and hell at all, and some do not believe at all in God. Many believers say that religion is no longer needed in order to be saved. You just have to accept Jesus Christ as your Lord and Savior and instantly you will be saved.

During the Christian dispensation, Judaism still existed as it was the religion that the Israelites or Hebrews brought from their race . When Jesus Christ preached the gospel, the converts in the land became Christians. The church of the first born in the wilderness which was lost had to be rebuilt and gathered by our Lord Jesus Christ. That is why, the Christ was sent by Father God to save them and the Gentiles. Gentiles are those people born out of Israel. Gentiles are receiver of God's promise of salvation through Jesus Christ. Jesus Christ is the head of the church . This is testified in Matthew 16:18 which reads," And I say unto thee that thou art Peter and upon this rock I will build my church; and the gates of hell shall not prevail against it." Doesn't this verse prove that our Lord Jesus Church would re build the church? You may ask, why does Christ have to rebuild the church if there was already a church ? Jesus Christ would rebuild the fallen church of the first born upon the rock.

Who is the rock? The rock refers to Jesus Christ who is the head of the church. This is testified in Ephesians 2:20, which reads " and are built upon the foundation of the apostles and prophets Jesus Christ himself being the chief cornerstone."According to the bible, the Lord God was the one who built the church for his people and this can be read in Psalm 127 which reads, " Except the Lord build the house, they labor in vain that build it; except the Lord keep the city; that watchman waketh but in vain." You can read the underlined phrase affirming, except the Lord builds the house(i.e. church), those men who build and are trying to establish their own churches are building them in vain or nothing. In other words, He is the only authority sent by God to re-build the church because the original Church of God which God built was lost.

The original members of the Church of God were the chosen few and the faithful firstborn church of Israel who were scattered and disappeared on earth because they were persecuted and some were even killed while the others who disobeyed and fell away became sinners. In other words, the church where we get together and associate with to worship God must be the Church that God built until the time our Lord Jesus Christ re built it. But, how is that? Where is that original church that God and Lord Jesus Christ built? How can we be part of that church that God had built if it is already gone or have long been lost for thousands of years? The bible teaches again that the church's name is the Church of God.

In I Thessalonians 2:14 says, " For ye, brethren, became followers of the churches of God which in Judea are in Christ Jesus: for ye also have suffered like things of your own country-men, even as they have of the Jews:"We may become part of that original Church of God in the bible by cleaving to what is good as instructed by the bible in Romans 12:9 which reads, " Let love be without dissimulation. Abhor that which is evil; cleave to that which is good." People who want to cleave with it must obey and believe in the doctrines of that church in the bible. In our dispensation, Jesus Christ must be the head of church as taught by the bible in Colossians 1:18, which says, " and he is the head of the body, the church; who is the beginning, the firstborn from the dead; that in all things he might have the pre-eminence." Therefore, there is no other head of the church , but our Lord Jesus Christ.

We shall know the true and original name of the church as the Church of God in 1Timothy 3:15 which reads, " but I tarry long that thou mayest know how thou oughtest to behave thyself in the house of God which is the church of the living God, the pillar and ground of the truth." In other verses of the bible, the official name of the church is " Church of God." This can be read for clarification in 1Corinthians 1:2 which reads, " Unto the church of God which is at Corinth." While there are so many names of church today, we should be aware if their teachings are the genuine teachings of the Christ because there is only one source of original teachings of the Christ, and that is from the chosen people , from the Church of God.

The apostle Paul, even mentioned the true church of God in I Corinthians 15:9 which says, " For I am the least of the Apostle, that am not meet to be called an apostle because I persecuted the Church of God." This verse testifies that Paul persecuted the Church of God when he was still in the religion of Judaism and was not yet a

Christian convert. While there is only one genuine and true Church of God, it follows that the teachings of God they impart to the people are biblically true and infallible. This is proven by the member of the true church in I Thessalonians 2:32-4." For our exhortation was not of deceit, nor of uncleanness, nor in quite, but as we were allowed of God to be put in trust with the gospel even so we speak, not as pleasing men, but God which tieth our hearts. Where is that church of God that the apostle Paul was part of ? Does it still existing and teaching the same as it was thousands of years ago?

The church of God is still existing today , but you should be aware of the teachings if it is the genuine teachings of the Christ in the bible. There are many similar names of the churches claiming to be the original church. To determine if the teachings are genuine, test if the teacher is teaching the infallible words and if the teachings are really happening. Test the spirits if it is of God as commanded in I John 4:1 which says, " Beloved, believe not every spirit, but try the spirits whether they are of God; because many false prophets are gone out into the world."Are believers obliged to be part of the church of God? Yes. The bible instructs believers to be part of the church of God. This is testified in Romans 12:9 which reads, " Let lover be without dissimulation. Abhor that which is evil; cleave to that which is good.' Notice the underlined phrase. *Cleave* refers to joining or becoming part of that which teaches good or the one that teaches the true teachings of God in the bible.

In other words, if you realize that you have been part of a false church that is not being taught in the bible, you are, of course, being taught to leave that church as commanded in the bible in 2Corinthians 6:14-17 which say, "Be ye not unequally yoked together with unbelievers; for what fellowship hath righteousness with unrighteousness? And what communion hath light with darkness? And what concord hath Christ with Belial? Or what part hath he that believeth with an infidel? And what agreement hath the temple of God with idols? For ye are the temple of the living God; as God hath said, I will dwell in them, and walk in them and I will be their God, and they shall be my people." Does your church have common descriptions of the true church or does it follow the ways of the world where the teachings do not conform with the true teachings in the gospel? If you want to be part of the true church , cleave to that one that teaches good and you will become God's people.

In Defense Of The True Teachings Of The Christ

Did you know that the Apostle Paul was the only apostle of the Christ, who received heavenly learning when his spirit was taken up to third heaven by God and experienced things that were not ever heard and learned by any prophets, apostles and servants in the bible? The Apostle Paul was given the wisdom and secret knowledge that neither Peter and other disciples nor Angels , nor Moses and all the prophets, the bible ever had did not receive. Paul, was the man referred to in the New Testament that was taken by God in spirit to third heaven to receive the teachings. Let us read 2Corinthians 12:2 " I knew a man in Christ above fourteen years ago, (whether in the body, I cannot tell; or whether out of the body, I cannot tell: God knoweth;) such a one caught up to the third heaven." Is it bad, unbiblical and unethical to debate with non-believers and religious fanatics about the true teachings of the Christ? – NO. Did disciples Paul, and Stephen confronted and debated with their religious adversaries in order to defend the teachings of the Christ to non-believers who tried to question them? -Yes. It is attested in Acts 6:9 which says, " Then there arose certain of the synagogue, which is called the synagogue of the Libertines, and Cyrenians, and Alexandrians, and of them of Cilicia and of Asia, disputing with Stephen. And they were not able to resist the wisdom and the spirit by which he spake." The said religious organizations during those days were all non-Christian believers who criticized the faith that

Paul and Stephen were preaching. Those were the sects that believed in Judaism.

According to Acts 9:22, reads, " But Saul (Paul)increased the more in strength, and confounded the Jews which dwelt at Damascus, proving that this is very Christ" Therefore, this verse explains how Paul ,who was called Saul defended his faithful stand on the Christ against the Jews which was his former religion. It is not ridicule to debate and defend your faith in the Christ as long as it is peaceful, non-violent, observing sportsmanship and for the sake of declaring your adversaries, the real teachings of the Christ. But, if the parties in the debate who would like to question your faith in the Christ are violent, harmful and with malicious intention, do not engage with them.

However, beware of false teachings as the bible warns us because many acting in true-Christian faith may mislead you. 1Timothy 6:3-4 says, " if any man teach otherwise, and consent not to wholesome words, even the words of our Lord Jesus Christ, and to the doctrine which is according to godliness he is proud, knowing nothing, but doting about questions and strife of words, whereof cometh envy, strife, railings, evil surmising," Another verse in Colossians 2:8, says, " Beware lest any man spoil you through philosophy and vain deceit, after the tradition of men, after the rudiments of the world, and not after Christ."

CHAPTER 3

Distinction Of The Creators

Distinction of God from the Son

Many religious groups and people believe that God and Jesus Christ are One in their beings, and that Jesus Christ is also the God. The same recognition for the Holy Spirit who, according to those who do not really know their distinction is also the God. In other words, the three persons in one being. They sum up the three into the so-called Trinity. There is no such thing as trinity in the bible. What we must understand is that the Father, the God- head, is the most powerful and Supreme God while the Son Jesus Christ is the God who was sent by the Father to save mankind on earth. Many believers do not distinguish one from the other, but people just understand that they are only One being or three in one. We have to distinguish one from the other in order to know who God is, and who our Lord Jesus Christ is, and who the Holy Spirit is. You may notice the distinction of the three is clearly specified in the bible as you read along the verses in each chapter. If you will not notice the distinction while reading the verses, then you will not be able to distinguish them as to their authority and lordship.

Certain verses that will distinguish the three Gods attest to their degree of authority and lordship that identifies or separates one from the other. Noticeably, in one scenario in the bible, when Jesus Christ was in the cross with His last Words, in John 17:1 reads, " *These words spoke Jesus, and lifted up his eyes to heaven, and said, Father, the hour is come; glorify thy Son, that thy Son also may glorify thee*" In this scenario, Jesus Christ lifted up his eyes to heaven as he called God in heaven. If God the Father is also the Son, Jesus Christ, why did He look up in heaven and called God. It is obvious that He was calling another Being in heaven. If they were Ones in being, of course, Christ did not have to look up and call God in heaven, instead He would just simply whisper and call for Himself alone because they were Ones, the others being inside His being already.

In this scenario, we apparently noticed and concluded that They are not in One Being, rather they are separate Beings and distinctive one from the other. This simply and obviously means, that God, the Father and the Son are different beings and we can say that they differ in the degree of authority if They are separate Beings because They are Gods. This allegation is proven and attested in the book of John 14:28, reads," *Ye have heard how I said unto you, I go away and come again unto you. If ye loved me, ye would rejoice because I said, I go unto the Father, for my Father is greater than I.*" In this verse, Jesus Christ said that He would go unto the Father and that the Father is greater than He. This means that the Father is in a higher authority than the Son. Jesus Christ himself as said in another verse that the One that sent Him is greater than the One that is Sent. The book of John 13:16 reads," *Verily, verily, I say unto you, the servant is not greater than His Lord; neither He that is Sent greater than He that sent Him.*"

Because Jesus Christ was sent by the Father as Savior of mankind, He himself would give those whom He saved to the Father. Referring to the book of John 17:11, " *And now I am no more in the world, but those are in the world, and I come to thee, Holy Father keep through thine own name those who thou hast given me, that they may be as one as We are One.*"" You may probably say that the Father is also the Son in the following verse, while the Son is also the Father at the same time upon reading this; John 10:30, "*I and my Father are One.*". *Many people misinterpret this verse because they out rightly interpret the verse as they read it verbatim. "I and the Father are One.*" Others believe in their understanding that because the verse says "I and the Father are One", they will conclude now that the Father is also the Son; and the Son is also the Father. No. It is a wrong notion.

If we shall ask a question: How did they become One,? Are they One in Being? The answer is: They are not One in being nor will they be Ones in the degree of lordships. Let us cite an instance of Oneness in other aspects, like the marriage of a man and a woman. Once they are married, the two become one" This means that husband and wife will become one , one is what? One in their obligations as couples, one in the flesh when they mate and produce children, one in richness and poorness, one in family bearing. John cannot become James while James cannot become John. Therefore, in what aspect did the Father and the Son become One?

Let us read John 10:28-29, " *And I give unto them eternal life; and they shall never perish, neither shall any man pluck them out of my hand. My Father which gave them me, is greater than all; and no man is able to pluck them out of my Father's hand." These two verses will tell us where the Father and the Son have become One.* In verse, 28, *the Son expresses concern and plays a good shepherd as well as the Father.* In verse 29, *the Father is a good shepherd and so the same with the Son, for they are both caretakers of the flock.*

Christians are also one with one another in the spirit and faith. This is quoted in the book of the Philippians 1:27, "*Only let your conversation be as it becometh the gospel of Christ; That whether I come and see you, or else be absent, I may hear of your affairs, that ye stand fast in one spirit, with one mind striving together for the faith of the gospel.*" Let us read John 17:11 which says, " *And now I am no more in the world, but these are in the world, and I come to thee, Holy Father, keep through thine own name* those whom thou hast given me, that they may be one, as we are." The underlined phrase " that they may be one" refers to those people who have been saved and gathered by the Son on earth because they all believed in God.

They all have one common belief and doctrine about God. In the same way, that the Father and Son are one in their work and purpose for the salvation of men. Therefore, this will interpret that there is oneness in doctrine and belief only; and conclusively not oneness in being. Therefore, the Father is a separate being from the Son, as the Son is a separate being from the Father. Curious minds may even ask if God the Father has a Father. Let us see what the bible answers. In Isaiah 43:10 says, " *Ye are my witnesses whom I have chosen; that ye may know and believe me, and understand that I am he; before me there was no God formed, neither shall there be after me.*"

The verse is clearly testifying there was no God before our God, neither there will be no other God after Him. Therefore, God has no beginning and no end. *Remember* God is a Supreme Being and Creator. He is not created nor has He have any origin. Isaiah 55:8 says, " *For my thoughts are not your thoughts, neither are your ways my ways, saith the Lord.*" We should know that questioning God's origin is not good and makes us offender? The bible teaches us not to think what is beyond our imagination about God's origin. Romans 12:3 says, "*For I say, through the grace given unto me, to every man that is among you, not to think of himself more highly than he ought to think; but to think soberly, according as God hath dealt to every man the measure of faith.*" Therefore, No man should fathom and think about God's origin because it is an offense to cast doubt and question about God.

Distinction of Jesus Christ from the Holy Spirit

We have distinguished the Father from the Son according to the degree of authority and lordship which were all supported by verses. With this, we can now distinguish Jesus Christ from the Holy Spirit in the degree of lordship and authority. In this distinction, Jesus Christ is greater than the Holy Spirit. Let us read John 14:26, "*But the Comforter, which is the Holy Ghost, whom the Father will send in my name, he shall teach you all things, and bring all things to your remembrance whatsoever I have said unto you.*" In the said verse, the Father will send the Holy Ghost in Jesus Christ's name, wherein the Holy Ghost will act as Comforter and a teacher to bring all things to remembrance. We can recall that the Father is the Supreme Being among the three Creators. Now, Jesus Christ is the second higher in authority next to Father God who sent Him.

Therefore, Jesus Christ is greater than the Holy Spirit (Ghost) whom He sent by the Father. In the previous discussion, we said that the One who sends is greater than the One being sent. In this instance, Jesus Christ is proven to be greater than the Holy Spirit by reading, John 15:26, "*But when the Comforter is come, whom I will send unto you from the Father, even the Spirit of Truth, which proceedeth from the Father, he shall testify of me.*" The verse we read testifies that the Son sends the Comforter from the Father. This implies that Jesus Christ is greater than the Holy Spirit whom he sent from the Father.

The Three Creators are One in their duties and mission to mankind, however, they differ in the degree of authority as Gods. Why did I say they are Creators? Because from the beginning they were together in the creation. Let us read, Genesis 1:26, " *Then God said, Let us make man in our image, in our likeness...*" The pronoun "us" indicates that God was not alone. He was with somebody during the creation, and that was our Lord Jesus Christ. However, there is no such thing as Trinity in the bible and nowhere in the bible you can find that term used. The God who is the Most High among them all and above everything else in heavens and on earth will remain the Most High, whom the Son will also be subjected unto Him. Let us read, 1Cor.15:27-28, " *For he hath put all things under his feet. But when he saith, all things are put under him, it is manifest that he is excepted, which did put all things under him. And when all things shall be subdued unto him, then shall the Son also himself be subject unto him that put all things under him, that God may be all in all.*"

These verses only prove that all things will be subject and under God including Jesus Christ, the Son of God, who is also subject unto God in the times to come. Others perceive there is only one

God. Yes, there is only one Supreme and Most High God, and that is God the Father, while our Lord Jesus Christ, who is born of God is also God who will be sent back to earth in the last days to save mankind. However, as mentioned, the Holy Spirit of God was there also since the beginning but no farther accounts are written in the bible. In addition, the Holy Spirit has come to guide, comfort and make us recall things that we forget. The Holy Spirit is part of the God-head. John 16:13 says, " *Howbeit when he, the Spirit of truth is come, he will guide you into all truth: for he shall not speak of himself; but whatsoever he shall hear, that shall he speak, and he will show you things to come.*"

The Holy Spirit will also help us in our weaknesses when sent. If we cannot utter our prayers by mere groaning the Spirit understands and makes intercession for us. In Roman 8:26, which reads, "*Likewise the Spirit also helpeth our infirmities: for we know not what we should pray for as we ought: but the Spirit itself maketh intercession for us with groanings which cannot be uttered.*

Jesus Christ as God

***Is Jesus Christ God*?**

There may be some churches or religious groups, except non-christian churches who do not believe in Christ, who believe Jesus Christ is a mere human being and a prophet only , but some do not believe at all in God. The bible is an existing book that proves Jesus Christ is God. Let us read, I Timothy 3:16, " *And without controversy great is the mystery of godliness: God was manifest in the flesh, justified in the Spirit, seen of angels, preached unto the Gentiles, believe on in the world, received up into glory.*" Who was manifest in the flesh? Was he not Jesus Christ ? Who was sent by God on earth and born of flesh to save the world? The underlined statement clearly states that Jesus Christ was born of flesh. Who do you think was sent from heaven, but Jesus Christ ?Furthermore, the bible says in John 1:14, " *And the Word was made flesh and dwelt among us, (and we beheld his glory, the glory of the only begotten of The Father) full of grace and truth.*" Who is the Word that was made flesh ? Let us read John 1:1 " *In the beginning was the Word and the Word was with God and the Word was God.*"

The verse says, in the beginning was the Word which was made flesh, therefore, if the Word was made flesh, it should emanate from the flesh also which is the human being because it is flesh and blood. First, Jesus Christ was born of the Father God in the spirit because God is a spirit, and second, He was sent by God to earth in the flesh in order to live with human beings who are in the flesh. So he was born into flesh. Let us read *John 6:51-54*, " *I am the living bread which came down from heaven : if any man eat of this bread, he shall live for ever: and the bread that I will give is my flesh, which I will give for the life of the world. . The Jesus strove among themselves, saying, How can this man give us his flesh to eat? Then Jesus said unto them, verily, verily, I say unto you, except ye eat the flesh of the Son of man, and drink his blood, ye have no life in you. Whoso eateth my flesh, and trinket my blood, hath eternal life; and I will raise him up at the last day.*" In this verse the flesh that will be given to the world is life. It means that the man in the flesh who was sent from above was the Life and Savior of the world and verse 54 says, " *Whoso eateth my flesh hath eternal life. Is this literal ? This is not literal, shall men eateth the flesh of humans? No. Flesh being referred to eat in this verse is the Word of God that men should learn. These are the teachings of Christ that should be obeyed so that mankind would have eternal life.* Let us read *John 6:69*, " *And we believe and are that thou art that Christ, the Son of the living God.*" Conclusively, Jesus Christ is God as stated in this verse, for He is the Son of the living God, and whatever is born of God is God. God is a spirit. No flesh and blood shall come from heaven nor go up in heaven in flesh and blood, as what the bible says.

Those who believe that Jesus was only a man would quote a certain verse in the bible to strengthen their claim that He is a human being only, the verse in *John 8: 40*,reads " *But now ye seek to kill me, a man, that hath told you the truth...*" In this verse the underlined word "man" affirms their belief that Jesus is human, a real man whom the people wanted to kill. The question is, In this scenario, what was the status of Jesus Christ ? Was he in the Spirit or in flesh ? Certainly, He was physically in the flesh and blood.

However, if you will continue reading the next verses below, up to *John 8:42*, it says, " *Jesus said unto them, If God were your Father, ye would love me; for I proceedeth forth and came from God; neither came I of myself, but he sent me.*" In this verse Jesus revealed that he came from God, Jesus Christ was a person whom came from God and was born of flesh by human beings through Virgin Mary so he might live with people. He was a Spirit when He was with God in heaven and was sent to earth in the form of flesh.

God Begets His Son Jesus Christ

It would sound unfamiliar, bizarre or peculiar to all that man is conceiving and begetting children. It sounds impossible, but the thing is, it is real that man conceives and begets children, because we normally know only that the one conceiving and producing is the female. Why, is it not possible that male conceives and produces? Even the bible attests to this fact in *Psalms 94:9* " *He that planted the ear, shall he not see?*" Which male is conceiving and begetting? For example the sea horse under the depth of the waters is the conceiving and begetting its offspring. God the Father conceives His Son Jesus Christ by means of His mind, thus creating Him in the beginning. Hebrew 1:5, " For unto which of the angels said he at any time, Thou art my Son, this day have I begotten thee?" The Son was begotten in the beginning, *Proverbs 8:22, says* " *The LORD possessed me in the beginning of his way, before his works of old,* "

Thus, our Lord Jesus Christ who was begotten from the beginning is God because the one that is begotten of God is God. And His beginnings were attested in *Proverbs 8: 24-32,* " *When there were no depths, I was brought forth; when there were no fountain abounding with water, Before the mountains were settled, before the hills was I brought forth; while as yet he had not made the earth, nor the fields, nor the highest part of the dust of the world, When he prepared the heavens, I am there: when he set a compass upon the face of the depth; when he established the clouds above; when he strengthened the fountain of the deep; when he gave to the sea his decree, that the waters should not pass his commandment; when he appointed the foundation of the earth; then I was by him, as one brought up with him;"*

We may ask, when was God when he made His creation and in the beginning of the creation? God was in His habitable part of his earth. In other words, it is no ordinary earth like the one where man lives and inhabit now, but He was in his own earth. *Proverbs 8:31 " rejoicing in the habitable part of the earth."*

God, The Father of Lord Jesus Christ, The Supreme Savior

If we are to tackle about the issue of mankind's salvation, precisely there is a Savior. There is an act of saving and somebody is to be saved. We ought to know that if we are going to be saved spiritually, that is, during the last day on earth if we are still alive and when the Savior Jesus Christ comes, and if we are already dead, we will be risen from the dead to face judgment. Let us read the bible to know who shall we recognize as the Supreme Savior in this work of salvation. In the book of I Timothy 4:10 which reads, " *For themselves we both labor and suffer reproach, because we trust in the living God, who is the Savior of all men, specially to those that believe."*

The verse was told by St. Paul to Timothy. He said, "we labor and strive, that we have put our hope in the living God. This is no other than God the Father, who is the Savior of all men, especially to those who believe. The phrase used by Paul here is the Savior of all men. This refers to salvation from the beginning of the creation of man until the last man who will be under the generation of salvation. This is the work of the living God, to save all men in all generations.

Who is the living God? We must realize that in order to be saved, we must all accept Jesus Christ as Lord and Savior in the last days on earth, but the more we must know His Word and teachings in the bible because if we will just accept Jesus Christ without knowing his teachings, how do Christians follow his commandments. Where are Christians heading to ?

There could be many Christ-like pretenders out there proclaiming they are the Christ and teaching different teachings which come from their own. The bible warns us that there will be many false prophets that will come out of this world saying they are the Christ and will mislead many. So be warned of this scenario. We ought to know the teachings and commandments of the genuine Jesus Christ in the bible in order not to be misled. Otherwise, you salvation in the last day is also endangered. In other words, some present day Christians say that the living God is our Lord Jesus Christ. Is it really true that the living God referred to in the bible is Lord Jesus Christ?

Let us read the book of Matthew 16:16-17, reads, " *And Simon Peter answered , Thou art the Christ the Son of the living God."* And Jesus answered and said unto him, "*Blessed art thou Simon Bar-Jona; For flesh and blood hath not revealed in unto thee, but my Father which is in Heaven.*"In other words, the living God is referred to God, the Father of our Lord Jesus Christ who is in heaven during that time. However, as of this time they are now both in heaven. Therefore, if you will ask, how many Gods are there? The answer is, there are many Gods. But there is only one most powerful God, and that is God the Father. The Son Jesus Christ is the next God who is also a powerful God and Savior of mankind.

The Holy Spirit and the Spirits of God

The Spirit of God and the Holy Spirit play important roles in the creation. Ever since the creation of heaven and earth, the Creators which are composed of Gods, the Son, and the Holy Spirit were altogether. What verse in the bible testifies that they were altogether during the creation? Let us read, *Genesis 1:26, "And God said, let us make man in our image, after our likeness, and let them have dominion over the fish of the sea, and over the fowl of the air and over the cattle."* The pronouns, "us" and "our" are two subjects that point out more than two other beings performing the creation. The Spirit of God attests to the creation and his presence in *Genesis 1:1-2, " In the beginning God created the heaven and the earth, and the earth was without form and void; and darkness was upon the face of the deep. And the Spirit of God moved upon the face of the waters, And God said, let there be light, and there was light."*In the said verse, the where about of the spirit of God during the creation was identified; the Spirit was hovering over the surface of the earth. You may ask the where about of God at the moment of creation.

The bible tells that God during that event of creation was in His own earth. In other words, he was dwelling in His created earth which no one could locate nor was it told in the bible. Perhaps, in the universe also. There is no record revealed about their where abouts, so we will only read what is written in the bible. The bible tells us that we must not go beyond what is written in the bible. In *1Corinthians 4:6, "And these things, brethren, I have in a figure transferred to myself and to Apollos for your sakes; that ye might learn in us not to think of men above that which is written, that no one of you be puffed up for one against another."* With this revelation we are taught to quote verses that are written only in the bible. In the verse we read, it is proven that the Spirit of God is one of the Creators. Another verse proves that the Spirit was with the Creators, can be read in Psalm 104:30 " Thou sendest forth thy spirit, they are created; and thou renewest the face of the earth." The work of the Holy Spirit in this verse is clearly stated, that He changes the face of the earth. In other words, the Spirit was the one who shaped the mountains and beneath the seas.

When Jesus Christ finished his mission on earth, he went up to heaven and told his disciples and followers that he would ask the Father to send a Comforter to be with the disciples. Let us go over the verses in John 14:16-17, " And I will pray the Father, and He shall give you another Comforter, that he may abide with you forever; even the Spirit of truth; whom the world cannot receive because it seeth him not; neither knoweth him but ye know him for he dwelleth with you and shall be in you."One of the main missions of the Holy Spirit for being sent to the world is to guide the works of the disciples. The Comforter will be with those who will pursue the works of the Christ and the Apostles until the coming of the Son of God, The true servants of God will be able to speak by the power and move of the Holy Spirit. Every word that they will say will come from heaven through the Spirit that is with them. We can read this testimony in John 16:13 that reads, "

How be it when he; the Spirit of truth has come he will guide you into all truth; for he shall not speak of himself; but whatsoever he shall hear, that shall he speak; and he will show you things to come."In other words, the Holy Spirit will move to speak to the Christians to relay the message from heaven. It is not from the will of men they will speak but by the power and moving of the Holy Spirit. The verse testifying this allegation can be read in II Peter 1:21 which reads, " For the prophecy came not in old time by the will of man; but holy men of God spake as they were moved by the Holy Ghost." In this verse, it is said that even the things to come will be revealed by the Spirit to the followers of Christ that is from God.

A servant has the Spirit of God when he walks not by the flesh but by the spirit. Everything changes in him. The way and manner he speaks are full of wisdom and knowledge. As one verse in the bible say, " When you are in Christ you are a new creation the old things have passed and the new ones have come." This testifies that when you are in Christ, you are a man of God. In Romans 8:16 reads, " The

Spirit itself beareth witness without spirit, that we are the children of God." The spirit that is in us will testify to our spirit that we will not walk in the flesh because the flesh sins. This is the truth in Romans 7:25, " I thank God through Jesus Christ our Lord, so then with the mind I myself serve the law of God; but with the flesh the law of sin."If a Christian is holy and righteous the Holy Spirit will be with him to guide and comfort him in all his life, and the knowledge and things he should know shall be put into his mind

On the other hand, Holy men bear good fruits and good things happen. And it shall manifest upon the holy men and people of God. This is the testimony in Galatians 5:22, " But the fruit of the Spirit is love joy, peace, long-suffering, gentleness, goodness, faith." There are many kinds of spirits that manifest in the flesh. Christians who win and turn away from the truth are told to restore in the faith. This is what the bible instructs us in Galatians 6:1, " Brethren, if a man be overtaken in a fault, ye which are spiritual, restore such a one in the spirit of meekness; considering thyself lest thou also be tempted." In this verse the Apostle Paul commanded the brethren who are at fault be restored to the spirit of meekness.

Now, we shall say that the flesh and the spirit are in contrast with each other. Otherwise, if one prevails over the other, the other may abide. This what we can read in Galatians 5:16-17, " This I say then, walk in the Spirit, and ye shall not fulfill the lust of the flesh. For the flesh lusteth against the Spirit, and the spirit against the flesh; and these are contrary the one to the other; so that ye cannot do the things that ye would." The Holy Spirit is sent to make us remember the things we should do and lead us to the right path in our lives. We can read this in John 14:26," But the comforter which is the Holy Ghost, whom the Father will send in my name; he shall teach you all things, and bring all things to your remembrance, whatsoever I have said unto you."Is there such a thing as " slain in the spirit?" There are religious groups that perform this kind of ritual. They lay hand on a person's head and by no reason a quivering person falls down in the arms of someone ready to catch behind her or him. Nowhere in the pages of the bible you can read an instance such as this one. There are evangelists who are allegedly filled with spirits as they drive out evil spirits from the body of an alleged demon-possessed person.

If these evangelists or preachers are really spirit-filled what kind of spirits do they have? Are they really preaching the true teachings of Christ? You may happen to ask this question to test the authenticity of their ministry. Who were those people doing these things in the past? Jesus Christ and His disciples did the healing and casting out of evil spirits during that time. Many wonders and miracles were done by them in the past. Today, wonders and miracles are done by modern day science and technology which are instrumental to make things possible. Finally, we should learn that God has seven Spirits. Let us read Isaiah 1:26, " And there shall come forth a rod out of the stem of Jesse and a Branch shall grow out of his roots; and the Spirit of the Lord shall rest upon him, the spirit of wisdom and understanding, the spirit of counsel and might, the spirit of knowledge and of the fear of the Lord." Did you know that God also sends evil spirits to men? This is what the bible tells in Judge 9:22-23. " When Abimelech had reigned three years over Israel, then God sent an evil spirit between Abimelech and the men of Shechem; and the men of Shechem dealt treacherously with Abimelech."

There are reasons why God send evil spirit to men, it is precisely for good and discipline of men. Like what happened to Saul of Israel when an evil spirit put him into trouble. Let us read I Samuel 16:14-15 which say, " But the Spirit of the Lord departed from Saul and an evil spirit from the Lord troubled him." And Saul's servants said unto him, Behold now, an evil spirit from God troubleth thee." But we should understand that if we are obedient to God. He will give us good spirits. He will pour out his spirits to his people as what the bible tells in Proverbs 1:23, " Turn you at my reproof behold, I will pour out my spirit unto you." In this verse a spiritual man is given the knowledge by God through the spirit.

Did the bible tell us that Jesus Christ is the same yesterday, today and forever? If he is the same today Is He still doing miracles? The answers to these questions are Yes. The reason why these questions are asked is that there are allegedly charismatic servants who are performing the works of the Apostles today. The driving out of evil spirits and healing of the sick and some are even trying to raise the dead. They claim that these works are still in effect today. Some of them may even inhibit you from taking medicines and seeing doctors. Religious people must realize that modern products of science and technology are the people behind such as doctors and scientists are all instrumental to accomplish good works on mankind.

Do you know that advance technology has been foretold in the bible? Let us read Daniel 12:4." But thou, Oh Daniel, shut up the words, and seal the book, even to the time of the end; many shall run to and fro, and knowledge shall be increased." Running to and fro refer to the modern day means of transportations such land vehicles, air craft, sea craft, and even space craft. This is apparently the product of man's growing knowledge. These things are instrumental also for man's welfare and good. People can go to other places through these metal objects and machines. People should not be misled from others' baseless beliefs that advance technology is the work of the devil. The proof that knowledge of men will advance is the discovery of modern things today while men continue to explore the wonder of science for mankind benefit. Iron was discovered by men to serve as men's tool for survival.

Knowledge advances, metal or iron has been a very crucial component in men's undertakings and progress. Men will be very busy as they go to and fro. They have discovered flying machines and consequently, they also developed weapons for men's destruction as time passes by. Men's knowledge is growing tremendously fast. Let us read the verse in Ecclesiastes 10:10, " If the iron be blunt, and he do not whet the edge, then must he put to more strength; but wisdom is profitable to direct." This is one proof that prophecies in the bible are coming to reality and fulfillment.

God does not change. He is the same yesterday, today and forever. He does wonders and miracles. One miracle is our daily survival ; our going to and fro everyday without being harmed and yet, still alive. Are they not miracles for us ? With these instances, we can prove that God is same yesterday, today, and forever. The truth about this is that the law in the past is already changed. The change in the law of the past can be read in Hebrew 7:12, which reads, " For the priesthood being changed, there is made of necessity a change also of the law." Hebrew 6:1-3 read, "

Therefore, leaving the principles of the doctrine of Christ, let us go on unto perfection; not laying again the foundation of repentance from dead works, and of faith toward God, of the doctrine of baptisms and of laying on of hands, and of resurrection of the dead, and of eternal judgment. And this will we do, if God permit." Therefore, men should advance as they leave the elementary teachings that have nothing to do today. It shall not effect today because the law has changed. The laying on of hands to the sick and other works that are commanded to be abandoned should be adhered to and follow the teachings of Christ today.

Men Are Called Gods

As you may know from the bible, there are many gods being mentioned in the books. The bible asserts the existence of other gods. In Philippians 3:19, " *whose end is destruction, whose god is their belly, and whose glory is in their shame, who mind earthly things.*" This verse refers to alleged servants of God, whose bellies have become their god because undeniably ,they keep enriching themselves without feeding their flock at the expense of their followers. Even during the time of Jesus Christ there were already priests, teachers and professed servants of God who enriched themselves but did not mind feeding and helping their followers. The bible warns us of these false prophets nowadays, in Isaiah 56:11 which reads, " *Yea, they are greedy dogs which can never have enough, and they are shepherds that cannot understand; they all look to their own way, every one for his gain, from his quarter.*"

These self-professed preachers and false prophets know nothing and cannot understand but to gain for themselves, and yet do not anything about the Word of God. They only know their routine works and even memorize what to preach as they prophesy in the congregation and yet it their prophecies are not happening because they are fake teachers. Do not be misled and be wise, the bible says. Ask them about the teachings of Christ in the bible, hence instructed by the bible in Haggai *2:11,* " *Thus saith the Lord of hosts; Ask now the priests concerning the law, saying,*"

The law that is asked us to ask to the priests (preachers, evangelists and pastors) is the teachings of Christ. If they cannot exactly answer about the written Word, then you begin to doubt that he or she is not a real servant of Christ. Try to monitor his ways and manners of living and you may identify who she or he is. There are three supernaturally powerful beings called God in the bible and as we have already learned and known they are the same Gods yesterday, today and forever. On the other hand , God has created other gods which do not possess supernatural powers. Since God is the Supreme God of all, he is the overall authority and judge in the midst of other gods.

The book of Psalm 82:1 says, "*God standeth in the congregation of the mighty; he judgeth among the gods.*"Human beings are called god, if they were born of God. We can all be called gods, if we are children of God. This is what the book of Psalm 82:6 says," *I have said, ye are gods and all of you, are children of the Most High."* This verse refers to men of God who are said to be gods and children of God, who really obey the laws of God. They are those who have received the teachings of Jesus Christ, and walking in the Spirit of God. Jesus Christ in a given situation in the bible told the people that men are gods, too. This means that men if were born of the Spirit of God will become children of God. In John 10:34-35, "Jesus *answered them, Is it not written in your law, I said, Ye are gods . if he called them gods, unto whom the word of God came, and the Scripture cannot be broken."*

In one scenario in the bible, Moses was made and called god by God. This is attested in the book of Exodus 7:1 reads," *And the Lord said unto Moses, See I have made thee a god to Pharaoh, and Aaron they brother shall be they prophet."* However, men have become selfish; for they do not really serve the real Most High God, but themselves. In the book of Romans 16:18, reads, "*For they that are such serve our Lord Jesus Christ, but their own belly; and by good words and fair speeches deceive the hearts of the simple."* These facts that are quoted are all derived from the bible as commanded and told by God.

It would be very unusual and seem muddling if we know there are many gods, however, one should learn and be enlightened to the fact that it is no ordinary fact and no wonder because thousands of years ago, there were many pretenders who emerged to be good men of God and what more in this present generation there are many who appear before men to be prophets of God and even introduce themselves as the Christ. People should not be misled upon knowing the facts from the bible that even Satan is called the god of this world, *2 Corinthians 4:4* " *in whom the god of this world hath blinded the minds of them which believe not, lest the* light of the glorious gospel of Christ, who is the image of God, should shine unto them."

CHAPTER 4

The Christ Of The Bible

Who is the Christ according to the bible? Christ means the Anointed One. Jesus Christ, the Son of the living God. St. Peter was speaking and said, "You are the Christ, the Son of the living God." What was the answer of Christ in this statement of St. Peter? Let us continue reading verse 17 of the book of Matthew 16, " *Jesus replied, Blessed are you , Simon, son of Jonah, for this was not revealed to you by man, but my Father in heaven.*" Take note that our Lord Jesus Christ told Peter the phrase, "Blessed are you Simon, son of Jonah, for this was not revealed to you by man, but my Father in heaven.

What was the meaning of the article this in this phrase? It means the recognition of Peter of Christ as the Son of the living God, who was not revealed by flesh and blood of man, but by the Father in heaven. That is why this Christ who is called the Son of the living God has a Father in heaven. Why must we know these facts from the bible? It is because in the book of 1Timothy 4:10, Paul said ," That we have put our hope in the living God, who is the Savior of all men, especially those who believe."

We give credit to our Lord Jesus Christ for saving us in the last days on earth as we wait for his return and much more we should give credit to the One who sent Him here on earth, the living God, the Father of our Lord Jesus Christ, who is the overall Savior. When the Son saves mankind then He would now deliver them to God the Father who will now become the Savior of all, with whom all and even the Son will be under His authority.We must understand that Christ is our mediator between God and men.

The book of 1Timothy 2:3-5 reads," *This is good, and pleases God our Savior, who wants all men to be saved and to come to a knowledge of the truth, for there is one God and one mediator between God and men, the man Christ Jesus.*" In these testimony of the preceding verses about the truth on Saviors, we now realize that we need to know and read the Word in the bible because it is not enough to say literally, to accept Jesus Christ in order to be saved. We need to know the law to be obeyed and known Him better.

Are we opposed when we say that our Lord Jesus Christ is a Savior?

Definitely, No. He is a Savior of mankind sent by God on earth and died for us . In the last day He will return to save mankind.

Life Is What We Maketh

Does God destine man's future? Man's thinking attitude towards his future should be analyzed and studied. People believe that fate of man is already pre-determined since birth. According to some people's insight , the fate of man has already been prepared and pre-determined, may it be good or bad. And that it has been destined by God that the future of a man is fixed to happen while he lives on earth. But this kind of notion is wrong. We should realize that man makes his destiny and future while keeping himself to survive the rigors of life on earth.

Literally, life may be good or bad according to the one who makes it. In reality, man does not know what lies ahead. This is proven in Hebrew 9:27, "*Just as man is destined to die once, and after that to face judgm*ent." This verse is certain that man is destined to die once. Precisely all men will die, but we are not certain with anybody's future on earth. The fact is, God wants us to have good future and he does not want us to suffer in this troubled earth. And it is also a fact that man is the one who is going to make and mold his own future while on earth. He has two choices : to make good and to make things bad for himself. Let us read Deuteronomy 30:19 " *This day I call heaven and earth as witnesses against you that I have set before you life and death, blessings and curses. Now choose life, so that you and your children may live.*"

In the said verse, man's mind is programmed to choose life, meaning he has to exert effort to succeed in life and do good in order to live, however, if he makes things bad for himself, he will reap the fruit of its consequences. Man will eat the fruit of his labor. If he does not work, therefore, he will not eat and will be impoverished and ultimately succumbs to death. Whatever comes out of his endeavor will be what he would be in this life. As the famous English poet, William Shakespeare said, " *Life is what we make it*" He even described life as like a stage where every man shall play a part. Whoever is strong and endures life's struggles survives. The weak is pathetically understood to give way.

The young ones take over the work of the old ones so that life may move on. For this reason, there is the existence of the rich and the poor on earth. The book of Proverbs 22:2 says, " *Rich and Poor have this common: The Lord is the Maker of them all." Perhaps some people may ask,* " Why are there rich and poor on earth?" Why not all are created rich so that everybody is happy? The answer is logical; if there are no poor, nobody will work, nobody will produce something to eat, something to serve us, and something that will keep alive and going. How shall we survive on earth if both things do not exist?

Not all shall be rich and not all shall be poor. The poor shall always work to lift up their status in life as there are always poor to come, while the rich shall also struggle to preserve their wealth and make their lives worth living. They will enhance their wealth for the benefit of the poor. The rich are also working and serving others, like the poor who also do their part. Everything on earth has its purpose that it may serve for the benefit of both parties. If nobody studies, nobody advances, that is why it is instructed in the bible that we serve one another. God permits men to explore everything for their benefit. The only thing that is pre-determined on earth is death.

Death is the only circumstance that is certain on earth. Everyone will die in his own time. Every human shall die along the way as he makes his living but it is not ascertained when it would happen. Some die young and some die old according to his circumstance. If God destines man to die would He change what He had destined? The answer is Yes. A certain verse will prove that the pre-determined death of man could be changed by God. Let us read, Isaiah 38:1-7, " *in those days Hezekiah became ill and was at the point of death. The prophet Isaiah son of Amos went to him and said, This is what the Lord says, "Put your house in order because you are going to die; you will not recover.*" Hezekiah turned his face to the call and prayed to the Lord. "*Remember, Oh Lord,* how I have walked before you faithfully and with wholehearted devotion and have does what is good in your eyes, and Hezekiah wept bitterly."

Then the word of the Lord came to Isaiah: Go and tell Hezekiah, this is what the Lord, the God of your father David says: I have heard your prayer and seen your tears: I will add fifteen years to your life. And I will deliver you and this city from the hand of the king of Assyria. I will defend this city. This is the Lord's sign to you that the Lord will do what he has promised." In these verses God changed the scheduled death of Hezekiah by adding fifteen years to his life. God has the sole authority to change things as He wills it. To have lengthy life on earth, we must fear God as what this verse tells in Proverbs 10:27, "

The fear of the Lord adds length to life, but the years of the wicked are cut short."There are people whose future on earth are already pre-destined as their destination is determined by God. It means they are chosen or pre-selected by God to do certain things on earth. Who are they? They are the sent or messengers of God. In the past, the prophets were destined to do the work as prophet of God even before they were formed in their mother's womb they were appointed in the right time to be prophet.

Let us read, Jeremiah 1:5, " *Before I formed thee in the belly I knew thee; and before thou camest forth out of the womb I sanctified thee and I ordained thee a prophet unto the nations.*" Even the apostle Paul had pre-determined destination to become an apostle of Christ. Before he was in the religion of the Jews (Judaism), he persecuted and even killed Christians but when he was called to serve God he was converted to Christianity and became an Administrator of the Church of the Living God.

However, ordinary people were given free will to choose which kind of life they wanted to live on and enter into for their future. We all don't know what lies ahead of us. You may be rich today, but tomorrow you may find yourself poor. You may be strong today, but tomorrow you find yourself sick or bed-ridden. Life is like a mist, according to the bible. Now you see him, now you don't. You may not be able to tell also what kind of a person you could be tomorrow. But there are some men who had been given assurance from their mother's womb of what they would be in the future. Paul, for example was chosen and was destined to be a disciple before he was an enemy of the Gospel. In *Galatians 1:13-15*, " *For ye have heard of my conversation in time past in the Jew's religion, how that beyond measure I persecuted the church of God, and wasted it, and profited in the Jew's religion above many my equals in mine own nation, being more exceedingly zealous of the traditions of my fathers. But when it pleased God, <u>who separated me from</u> my mother's womb, and called me by his grace.*"

The Impossible Thing With God

There are many religious groups today that say nothing is impossible with God. The verse in the bible is in Matthew 12:41, " *Jesus looked at them and said. With man this is impossible, but with God all things are possible.*" It is really the truth that everything undoubtedly happens by God's will. If we shall look at the other verse, it appears that something is impossible with God. Let us read the verse in Titus 1:2, " *a faith and knowledge resting on the hope of eternal life, which God, who does not lie promised the beginning of time.*" In the said verse, there is something which God is impossible to do and that is, to tell a lie. Unlike men who lie, God never lies as He is true in everything. Romans 3:4 says, " *Not at all ! Let God be true, and every man a liar. As it is written: So that you may be proved right in your words and prevail in your judging.*

Even Jesus Christ did not lie nor sin. This is proven in a certain verse in 1Peter 2:21-22, "*he committed no sin, and no deceit was found in his mouth.*" We can out rightly say that men are liars. These liars are people who are under curse of sin and who continually sin for their father is a liar. Be warned of the emerging false prophets and self-professed Christian pastors, evangelists and preachers because they might be teaching a different doctrine other than that of the doctrine of Christ in the bible.

The bible in Galatians 1:8 tells us, " *But though we, or an angel from heaven, preach any other gospel unto you, let him be accursed.*" The instruction in this verse is strictly to be enforced while we are warned of those false teachings not pertaining to teachings of Christ. " Let those false prophets be accursed accordingly!"

Liars are rampant nowadays, these false prophets are sowing their false teachings and some continue their wicked ways as they serve their father, the devil. Let us read John 8:44, " *You belong to your father, the devil and ;you want to carry out your father's desire. He was a murderer from the beginning, not holding to the truth, for there is no truth in him. When he lies, he spoke his native language, for he is a liar and the father of lies.*" Beware that you are not deceived.

How will you know that they are of God or not ? John 7:17-18 say, " *If any man will do his will, he shall <u>know of the doctrine</u>, whether it be of God, or whether I speak of myself. He that speaketh of himself seeketh his own glory; but he that seeketh his glory that sent him, the same is true, and no unrighteousness is in him.*" In other words, they speak for themselves basically founded by their own knowledge, imagination and notion. We should all be reminded that wicked men do not stop from deceiving and sowing wickedry and they even act as true or real people like their father, the devil acts also like an angel of light. 2 Corinthians 11:13 says, "

For such are false apostles, deceitful workers, transforming themselves into the apostles of Christ. And no marvel; for Satan himself is transformed into an angel of light."So, beware of the false prophets and workers acting as real but deceitful in their deeds and creeds. One way you can test them is by their own teachings if they are founded by the teachings of Christ. Be sure that every statement that they pronounce to you is attested by verses in the bible as you test the spirit.

Do not be comforted and persuaded by their sweet, flattery and self uplifting words but rather test the spirit that they bring and pronounce. Because when man comes to you with spiritual deliverance, we are already talking about our soul's salvation and this is a delicate issue to tackle. There is no such thing as instant salvation. Let us read I John 4:4 which says, " *Beloved, believe not every spirit, but try the spirits whether they are of God; because many false prophets are gone out into the world*"

When you are convinced by false teachings you have entrusted already your soul to a false prophet thereby you are led to death in the last day of judgment. Because when you are led by a false prophet both of you would plunge to the pit of burning lake of fire in the last day. It is not bad to see and listen to every teaching of any churches because in that manner you will be able to discern whether they are of God or not. By then, God will reveal to you according to His purpose in your life the truth if you continue to seek His word. Because hearing the word is the beginning of your wisdom and belief.

Misfortune Of Men

Why do crippled, ill-starred, deformed, and freak-looking men exist? They exist in order that God's power and work be revealed to all men. *John 9:3," Jesus answered, Neither hath this man sinned, nor his parents; but that the works of God should be made manifest in him."*We may wonder why God created all these things in men? We cannot question the one who created us. Can we question the Maker of everything that exists? Can a pot that man molds question, why has it been formed this way or that way? No. R*omans 9:20, "Nay, O man who are thou that repliest against God? Shall the thing formed say to him that formed it, Why hast thou made me thus? Hath not the potter power over the clay, of the same lump to make one vessel unto honor, and another unto dishonor?"*

Exodus 4:11, " And the LORD said unto him, Who hath made man's mouth? Or who maketh the dumb, or deaf, or the seeing, or the blind? Have not I the LORD?" Therefore, the LORD has the power to create all these things and makes things exist according to his will.

CHAPTER 5

Righteous Ways of Praying as Taught by the Christ

One of the teachings of the Christ during his time on earth which the present day Christians should do is the right way of praying. Perhaps, everyone is praying in his own desired way. We pray before eating and sleeping and even when we leave the house or somewhere down the road, However, Christ had instructions to men and women when praying. Man should observe due respect when praying. He should remove and avoid any head covering while woman must have covering in her head which is an observance of due respect in praying to God. This is written in 1Corinthians 11:4-5 which read," *Every man praying or prophesying having his head covered, dishonoreth his head; for that is even all one as if she were shaven.*"As these verses testify to the fact of Christ's command, the woman and man should observe and obey, so judge for yourselves as what the bible tells in 1Corinthians 11:13 which says, "*Judge in yourselves; it is comely that a woman pray unto God uncovered.*"

On the other hand, everyone is being asked to pray in designated places that is inside the room. The bible in one scenario, reveals those hypocrites in the past and present who pray in open places, in public where people could see them and in loud prayers so people could notice them. The bible teaches us to pray properly as what the book of Matthew 6:6 says, "*But thou, when thou prayest, enter into thy closet, and when thou hast shut thy door, pray to thy Father which is in secret, and thy Father which seeth in secret shall reward thee openly. The verse is self explanatory and understandable.*"

As we pray the righteous praying should be whole-hearted no matter if you cry because that is biblical. Let us read, Hebrew 5:7, "*Who in the days of his flesh, when he had offered up prayers and supplication with strong crying and tears unto him that was able to save him from death, and was heard in that he feared.*" Prayers must always be associated with thanksgiving because that is pleasing and one way of worshipping God. Let us read Philippians 4:6, " *Be careful for nothing; but in everything by prayer and supplication with thanksgiving let your requests be made known unto God.*" A Prayer of Thanksgiving is the most important part when praying.

Prayers Heard and Prayers Not Heard by God

If others have sinned against you, it is necessary to ask God that they may be forgiven but you should not harbor in your heart hatred nor let animosity dwell in you because if you don't forgive them you will not be forgiven by God. Matthew 6:14 says, " *For if ye forgive men their trespasses, your heavenly Father will also forgive you. But if forgive not men their trespasses, neither will your Father forgive your trespasses.*" God will not hear the prayers of a sinful person as what the bible tells in Lamentations 3:44, " *Thou hast covered thyself with a cloud, that our prayer should not pass through.*"

In other words, the prayers of sinners cannot reach God. Another reference verse tells us that God only hears the prayers of a righteous man, in Proverbs 28:9 says, " *He that turneth away his ear from hearing the law, even his prayer shall be abomination."Another verse in John 9:31 attests, "Now we know that God heareth not sinners; but if any man be a worshipper of God, and doeth his will, him he heareth."* The preceding verses are self-explanatory that prayers of a righteous man and a worshipper of God are heard.

Much more God will not hear our prayers when we use vain repetitions in praying. This is what the bible tells in *Matthew 6:7* which reads, " *But when ye pray, use not vain repetitions as the heathen do; for they think that they shall be heard for their much speaking. Be not ye therefore like unto them; for your Father knoweth what things ye have need of, before ye ask him.*" Now it is understood that God does not want repetitions in praying. In fact He knows the things we want even if we have not asked it from Him, yet.

But we should always pray to Him for whatever blessings we receive day and night. *Luke 18:1* says" *And he spake a parable unto them to this end, that men ought always to pray, and not to faint.*" The instruction says that we should always pray and do not faint. Faint here means do not neglect because the book of *I John 5:15* says," *And if we know that he hear us, whatsoever we ask, we know that we have the petition that we desired of him*".

First and important for us is to give thanks unto the Lord and even the Apostle Paul taught us to give thanks to the Lord. This is taught in *II Timothy 1:13* which says," *Paul, an apostle of Jesus Christ by the will of God, according to the promise of life which is in Christ Jesus. To this "I thank God, whom I serve from my forefathers with pure conscience that without ceasing I have remembrance of thee in my prayers night and day.*"How often shall we pray? According to the verse pray without ceasing and ceasing does not mean literal here. It means in the nighttime and day time only.

How Do We Pray And What Shall We Pray?

We should pray in this manner according to ***Matthew 6:9-13*** which read,

"Our Father which art in heaven,
Hollowed be thy name
Thy kingdom come
Thy will be done
In earth, as it is in heaven
Give us this day our daily bread
And forgive us our debts
As we forgive our debtors
But deliver us not into temptation
But deliver us from evil
For thine is the kingdom, and the power, and the glory forever, Amen.

However, in a given situation like for instance, when you are trapped in the midst of a traffic jam along the road and you ought to be in the office because of an urgent meeting with your boss, will you utter the same prayer? Not anymore, you will ask and pray that you get to your office on time for a meeting. You need not pray that way because prayer depends upon the demand of the circumstances and our God knows our circumstance and understands the prayer that we want to utter in a given situation. Prayer depends upon a given situation. If suddenly, an earthquake shakes the environment and everybody is panicky what prayer should you utter at that moment? Should you ask for food or forgiveness? Of course, not anymore. You may suddenly utter, a word, " God save us from this earthquake!" or " God please stop the earthquake!" or " Gold help us!"

When you pray, don't forget to give thanks to the Lord which is very necessary in order that we may always be blessed as we make know to Him our requests. *Philippians 4:6, " Be careful for nothing; but in everything by prayer and supplication with thanksgiving let your requests be made known unto God."*

Positions Of The Body When Praying

How Do We Position Ourselves When Praying? Normally, when we are in the room we pray sitting or kneeling on the floor and bow our head as we pray. But in some situations, Christians who cannot properly sit and kneel down because of physical problem may just position himself or herself in a position where he or she is comfortable for God knows your situation.

In addition, the normal and biblical form of prayer for Christians is that we may pray by facing our body flat on the floor and facing towards the ground or floor also because Jesus prayed that same position when He was in the garden of Gethsemane. He prayed fervently, while his body on the ground facing down. He wept when he prayed in the same manner that Christians pray with weeping and groaning solemnly.

How did Jesus position himself as he prayed? Let us read *Matthew 26:39," And he went a little further, and fell in his face and prayed, saying, O my Father, if it be possible, let this cup pass from me; nevertheless, not as I will, but as thou wilt."*

CHAPTER 6

Parts Of The Body That Incite Men to Sin

The Eyes and Hands

When praying we should realize that there are parts of our body that are exposed to sin which may drive us totally to dwell in sin. Because of these parts of our body we keep sinning and our prayers may not be heard. Why? Because they aggravate and even drive us to a filthy living .The bible warns us in *Matthew 5:29* which reads, " *And if thy right eye offend thee, pluck it out, and cast it from thee; for its is profitable for thee that one of thy members should perish, and not that thy whole body should be cast into hell.* " *And if thy right hand offend thee, cut it off, and cast it from thee; for its is profitable for thee that one of their members should punish, and not that thy whole body should be cast into hell."*

Should you pluck out your eyes because they keep you from sinning and your right hand drives you to sin? Should you cut it off literally to keep you away from sinning? Of course, not. Don't take those verses literally, otherwise you will be disabled to continue a normal and descent living and you find no more chance to spiritually renew yourselves. All you have to do is to keep yourselves out and abandon filthy activities in your life. Hold your hands and control your eyes from temptations. As we all know, it is easy to become Christian but we find a hard time living a Christian-like living. It is a daily struggle but eventually as you grow and become Spirit- filled you and I will learn to get hold of these things.

The Heart

The heart is part of the body that keeps men from sinning. The book of *Jeremiah 17:9*, tells us," *The heart is deceitful above all things, and desperately wicked: who can know it? I the Lord search the heart."* The Lord God knows if a person is hiding filthy thing in himself. We can hide nothing from God because He searches every man's heart.

The heart is a body part that keeps man's sin which others cannot see. The danger is, the heart keeps evil thoughts and plans dreadfully against an enemy. The heart in other words, is the habitat of all evil thoughts against men's enemies. All the filthy plots and evil thought are kept in the heart. The bible attest to this fact in *Matthew 15:19*, reads ,"*For out of the heart proceed evil thoughts, murders, adulteries, fornications, thefts, false witness, blasphemies.' These are the things which defile a man; but to eat without washing hands defileth not a man.*"

In the last line of the verse, it may be better for us to eat without washing the hands than keep all those evil thoughts in our hearts because you may not die without washing your hand but the worst thing that may happen is that you die a sinful life. Because of the evil heart God saw the wickedness of men through their hearts that He punished them by the great flood. The same thing may happen to men nowadays to be punished in different ways. But in the past, the first race of mankind was punished. Let us read the book of *Genesis 6:5*," *God saw that the wickedness of man was great in the earth, and that every imagination of the thoughts of his heart was only evil continually.*"

So God brought the Great Flood in the history of mankind and killed all living creatures. The aftermath was horrible and mournful that God said He would not punish mankind the same kind of punishment. *Genesis 6:6-7*" *Had it repented the Lord that He had made man on the earth , and it grieved Him at his heart. And the Lord said, I will destroy man whom I have created from the face of the earth; both man and beast , and the creeping thing, and the fowls of the air, for it repenteth me that I have made them.*"The promise of the Lord was symbolized by the appearance of the colorful rainbow. However, in the end of time mankind would not suffer the same punishment again, but will be destroyed by the blazing fire.(Revelation).

The Danger of Tongue

Tongue is another part of the body which can lead man to hell. The book of *James 3:6 reads, " And the tongue is a fire, a world of iniquity: so is the tongue among our members that it defileth the whole body and setteth on fire the course of nature; and it is set on fire of hell.*"The tongue is so little but it can lead us to trouble and makes things worst for us. It is a big problem that in its littleness it can create big fire or trouble. *James 3:5* says, " *Even so the tongue is a little member, and boasteth great things, behold, how great a matter a little fine kindleth.*"

Man may be able to tame the beast but our tongue is so wicked and poisonous that it cannot be tamed by anybody. The tongue can spark trouble and can curse others to a big mess. It can curse and bless others like what *James 3:7*,10 say, " *For every kind of beasts , of birds, and of serpents and of things in the sea, is tamed, and hath been tamed of mankind: but the tongue can no man tame: it is untruly evil, full of deadly poison . Out of the same mouth proceedeth blessing and cursing.*"

However, we can make our tongue useful and keep us upright if we hold it and keep it upright. The book of *Proverbs 15:1* reads, " *The tongue of the wise useth knowledge aright: but the mouth of fools poureth out foolishness.*"In the same manner we could avoid trouble with others if we hold our tongue. Evil tongue creates and spreads maligning words, a filthy gossip. Proverbs 11:9 says, "*A hypocrite with his mouth destroyeth his neighbor; but through knowledge shall the just be delivered.*"

There is no other way to stop the evil tongue but to stay pure and clean in the sight of the Lord by remembering His laws by reading and obeying the Word . It cleans us from all our inequities particularly the filthiness of the parts of our body that drive us to a sinful living. *John 15:3 says." Now ye are clean through the Word which I have spoken unto you.*"

Speaking in Tongues

In I Corinthians 14:27 says, " *If any man speak in an unknown tongue, let it be by two or at the most three and that by course, let one interpret*" The first apostles during the Pentecost spoke in tongues, because they were filled with the Holy Spirit. They spoke the tongues of many nations. Let us read the verse in Acts 2:4-6, " *And they were all filled with Holy Ghost, and began to speak with other tongues, as the Spirit gave them utterance. And there were dwelling at Jerusalem Jews devout men, out of every nation under heaven. Now even when this was noised abroad, the multitude came together, and were confounded because that every man heard them speak in his language.*"

In this situation the apostles spoke in tongues, meaning they were able to speak the languages of other nations like for example the native languages of the Parthians, Medes, Elamites, residents of Mesopotamia, Judea, and Cappadocia, Pontus and Asia. There were amazed upon knowing that everyone could speak in different languages which were not their native languages, and they understood each other's language.

These were the kinds of tongues they were able to speak in the Pentecost and not those unknown tongues that just come out from the mouth of the present-day performers. Let us read Acts 2:7-11, "*And they were all amazed and marveled, saying one to another, Behold, are not all these which speak Galileans? And how hear we every man in our own tongue, wherein we were born? Parthians, and Medes, and Elamites, and the dwellers in Mesopotamia, and in Judea, and Cappadocia, in Pontus, and Asia, Phrygia, and Pamphylia, in Egypt, and in the parts of Libya about Cyrene, and strangers of Rome, Jews and proselytes, Cretes and Arabians, we do hear them speak in our tongues the wonderful works of God.*"What should believers do when somebody speaks in tongue ? Let us read I Corinthians 14:28, " *But there be no interpreter, let him keep silence in the church: and let him speak to himself and to God.*" This verse tells us that there is no need to speak in tongues, but to keep quiet and speak to himself and to God.

This is an indication that there is a need for an orderly worship within the church. Like what this verse in the bible tells in I Corinthians 14:33, says, "*for God is not the author of confusion but of peace, as in all churches of the saints.*" Conclusively, speaking in tongues belongs to the instructions of the Old practice in the old church during the Pentecost. This is part of the law that was changed. In Hebrew 6:1-3 say, " *Therefore, let us leave the elementary teachings about Christ and go on to maturity, not laying again the foundation of repentance from acts that lead to death...*"

We can also refer to Hebrew 7:12, " *For when there is a change of the priesthood, there must also be a change of the law.*"It is a fact also that there are many religious groups in these days that exercise the casting out of evil spirits, diseases, and whatever kinds of spirits there could be. Do these things conform with the word of God in this present dispensation ? The answers can be read again in Hebrew 6:1-3, and Hebrew 7:12. which are often quoted due to the demand of the situation. In these verses, Christian –believers are instructed to abandon these teachings already due to the change of the law. The proper thing to do is to pray fervently to God to stop the nature's fury and the destructive calamity, heal diseases and ask Him to drive away all evil spirits or pray in the Name of Jesus to drive away filthy spirits around.

It is stated in Philippians 2:13, "*For it is God which worketh in you both to will and to do of his good pleasure*" In other words God will work to those righteous servants who are deserving in His sight, and that is according to what he wants them do. Servants do not have to perform spiritism that may cause others to stumble. What was taught in the bible when someone is sick? In James 5:14-16 read," *Is any one of you sick? He should call the elders of the church to pray over him and anoint him with oil in the name of the Lord. And the prayer offered in faith will make the sick person well; he will be forgiven. Therefore confess your sins to each other so that you may be healed.*

The prayer of a righteous man is powerful and effective."Again, anointing of oil means teaching the sick with the Word of God. By prayer and petition for the sick God may heal him. The elderly who shall pray should be clean and unblemished because God hears the prayer of a righteous person.

Food Served to Idols and the Forbidden Meat

Another sin against the Holy Spirit is the eating of foods offered to idols. It was forbidden by God to believers to keep themselves out of the food such as blood, or food with blood of any animals, and the meat of strangled animals. Let us read the book of *Acts 15:29*, "*that ye abstain from meats offered to idols, and from blood and from which if ye keep yourselves, ye shall do well, fare ye well*." The said verse testifies the fact about the abstention from eating the specified foods. In the past, God's command to his people was not to eat strangled animals but instead give it to those people who did not belong to the church or to His people. The book of *Deuteronomy 14:21* says, " *Ye shall not eat of anything that dieth of itself: Thou shall give it unto the stranger that is in thy gates, that he may eat it; or thou mays sell it unto an alien; for thou art a holy people unto the Lord thy God*."

You will feel and notice that God is keeping His people out of danger of committing sin. The strangulated animals can be given and sold by the Gentiles or people that do not belong to His flock or it may be sold by them to an alien. Nowadays, there still exists. His people in the Church who obey these laws. You may ask, are these laws in the past still existing and being applied nowadays? Definitely yes, because there are laws in the past that are still applicable to present day Christians and there are laws in the past that are no longer applicable today which were only applied during that time in the Old testament.

The Blood

God does not want us to eat blood because it is a symbol of our salvation and redemption from our sins. In *Leviticus 17:10-11* read," *For the life of the flesh is in the blood: and I have given it to you upon the altar to make an atonement for your souls; for its is the blood that maketh an atonement for the soul.*" The verse clearly reasons out why blood is forbidden by God to be eaten by believers or his people. Another verse in the bible which attests the significance of the blood in the remission of our sins can be read in *Hebrew 9:22* " *And almost all things by the law purged with blood; and without shedding of blood is no remission.*" Obviously, these idols or graven images of people of the past which caused them sin, are still being worshipped today by many people who had been blinded by false teachings.

However, aside from idols which unbelievers worship today are other sins of idolatry in which these idol worshippers shall be held accountable to God in the last day. What are these other sins of idolatry. Let us read *Colossians 3: 5-6* ," *Mortify therefore your members which are upon the earth; fornication, uncleanness, inordinate affection, evil concupiscence, and covetousness, which is idolatry: for which things' sake the wrath of God cometh on the children of disobedience.*"If idol worshippers would turn away from these despicable way of worship they will be forgiven. If they get enlightened and realized the truth they will be freed from the bondage of sin.

They just don't realize that graven images cannot do any harm against them if they throw and abandon it because they are just mere stones and piece of wood and some nowadays are made of plastic or resin materials. In *Proverbs 115: 4-7*. "*However, Jeremiah 10:5 proves they are nothing and can't do any harm . the verse reads, " they are upright as the palm tree, but speak not: they must needs be borne; because they cannot go. Be not afraid of them; for they cannot do evil, neither also is it in them to do good.*"

God is a jealous God. He does not want us to worship idols and any creations. God is a spirit and all who worship Him shall worship in spirit and truth. To prove this statement, let us read *John 4:23-24*, " *But the hour cometh, and now is, when the true worshippers shall worship the Father in spirit and in truth; for the Father seeketh such to worship him. God is a spirit; and they that worship him must worship him in Spirit and in truth.*"

The Sin of Adultery in the Spirit

Adultery in the spirit is a fellowship of believers with the religious practices of the unbelievers. This is another sin against the Holy Ghost which cannot be forgiven. If the believers who have received the doctrine of God concerning faith and yet have fellowship with the religious practices of the Gentiles, the former have sinned a worst sin that cannot be forgiven. In *I Corinthians 6:15-18* we read," *Know ye not that your bodies are the members of Christ? I then take the members of Christ, and make them the members of harlot? God forbid. What! Know ye not that he which is joined to a harlot is one body? For two saith he, shall be one flesh. But he that is joined unto the Lord is one spirit. Flee fornication. Every sin a man doeth is without the body; but he that committeth fornication sinneth against his own body.*" These verses warn the believers who are already in the faith to keep out from the sinful works of the world.

In other words, if you associate with unbelievers (Gentiles) or have fellowship with them do not do what they do particularly the don'ts or laws of God you have been taught of or do not perform things that you know will cause you to sin. Believers should observe carefully that they don't practice or perform the religious practices of the Gentiles, in particular, that may cause them sin.

Let us read *II Corinthians 6:14-18*, " *Be ye not unequally yoked together with unbelievers; for what fellowship hath righteousness with unrighteousness ? And what communion hath light with darkness? And what concord hath Christ with Belial? Or what part hath he that believeth with an infidel? And what agreement hath the temple of God with idols? For ye are the temple of the living God as God hath said, I will dwell in them, and walk in them, and I will be their God and thy shall be my people. Wherefore come out from among them, and be ye separate, saith the Lord, and touch not the unclean thing, and I will receive you, and will be a Father unto you, and ye shall be my sons and daughters, said the Lord Almighty."*

In the said verses, Believers are commanded to refrain from doing the practices of the unbelievers. Do believers forbidden to befriend and associate with unbelievers? Definitely, No. What is common and uncommon between believers and unbelievers? Can you associate light with darkness ? What concord does Christ have with Belial (Devil) ? Is there any agreement between the temple of God with Idols ? Your answers may be definite and certain .Believers should not commit adultery in the spirit, meaning , they should not perform the religious practices of the Gentiles or the unbelievers.

This is attested in *I Corinthians 6:15*, which reads, "*Know ye not that your bodies are the members of Christ? Shall I then take the members of Christ, and make them the members of a harlot? God forbid.*"

Therefore, it is clear that believers should not do the forbidden rituals of the unbelievers (harlot as referred by the bible), because their bodies are already members of Christ. If they do so, they will not be forgiven.

CHAPTER 7

Transgressions of Men

In the beginning the first man and woman sinned against God. The sin of disobedience, obviously was the first sin committed that caused the first human beings to be punished. Take note that our first parents, Adam & Eve sinned because they ate the physical fruit called Apple. In fact, they did not really ate apple when they sinned because apple during that biblical time apple was already being eaten as fruit by the Israelites. Adam & Eve sinned because they chose to commit sin which is the fruit of the tree of knowledge of good and evil, but not the tree of apple.

Let us read, *Genesis 2:16-17*, "*And the Lord God took the man, and put him into the garden of Eden to dress it and to kept it. And the Lord God commanded the man, saying, Of every tree of the garden thou mayest freely eat: but of the knowledge of good and evil, thou shalt not eat of it: for in the day that thou eatest thereof thou shalt surely die.*"

In other words, God gave us free will to choose between good and evil. If you choose evil, your life will be misled, astray and consequently, you end up destroyed ; but if you choose good, of course, you are not far from good but you are enlightened while you lead a right path to bright future and good living. We all know that sin has its re-compensation and that every sin that we make has to be accounted for in the end. To commit a sin is an inevitable act in this world. There are big or weighty sin and small or light sins that we commit in our lives. How do you know that when you repent your sins will be forgiven or are forgiven?

The bible answers, in *Psalms 32 :5* which says, "*I acknowledge my sin unto thee, and mine iniquity have I not hid. I said, I will confess my transgressions unto the Lord; and thou forgavest the iniquity of my sin.*" Therefore, acknowledge and confess your sins only unto the Lord, but to no man because we should realize that Christians commit sins, but we pray for forgiveness and do the same thing while still living. But for Christians, repeating the same sins would mean death in the end. He would not be saved and forgiven anymore. But, if you sin without any intention of committing it you may be forgiven. This is affirmed and cited in the bible.

The Sins Of Back Sliders

Back Sliders are those who have become believers but turned away from the faith they received as they do the same works of the world of unbelievers. There are reasons why they turned away from the faith. It may be because they could not resist the devil's calling; weak in their faith; they cannot bear the test in their lives and in their faith; they have not received the fruits of the Holy Spirit or they have not received the faith in Christ intentionally or truly; they got stumbled with other believers and other reason that may cause their turning back. They cannot resist the calling of the flesh. As the bible says, the spirit is willing but the flesh is weak.

The book of *Hebrews 6:4-6 read, "For its is impossible for those who were once enlightened; and have tasted of the heavenly gift, and were made partakers of the Holy Ghost, and have tasted the good word of God and the powers of the world to come, if they shall fall away, to renew them again unto repentance seems they crucify to themselves the Son of God afresh and put him to an open shame."* The fate of the back sliders may become worst because if they do worst things they will be condemned to spiritual death. When they turned away from their faith they have re-crucified the Son of God anew. It means they have put into shame the Son of God for what they did.

Back Sliders may be rebuked for wrongdoings so they may make up their minds and turn away from sinning. The bible teaches us in *Titus 3: 10 which reads, " A man that is a heretic, after the first and second admonition, reject; knowing that he that is such is subverted, and sinneth, being condemned of himself."* You may rebuke him or her one or two; and he or she does not listen reject and abandon him or her. You will not be held responsible for his infirmity Other back sliders may not be saved anymore if they continue in their evil ways until their end. They are like dogs which come back to its vomit. II Peter 2:20 says, "For if they have escaped the pollution of the world through the knowledge of the Lord and Savior Jesus Christ, they are again entangled therein, and overcome, the latter end is worse with them than the beginning."

The Two Kinds of Sins of Men

Mortal Sin

This is the kind of sin that sinful men cannot be forgiven anymore and literally in the end, sinners will be bound to damnation. We believe that if we sin and pray for forgiveness we are forgiven as the bible says, however, we should realize that there are sins that cannot be forgiven . Mortal sin is a fatal type of sin that even if somebody else prays for that sinner, he can no longer be saved. This is a very critical issue that believers should contemplate profoundly. Christians in the Church of God , the chosen Church know about this sin but there are those who do not know this mortal sin particularly those outside of the Church.

The sin against the Holy Spirit is the type of sin that cannot be forgiven. Our Lord Jesus Christ may forgive those sins against Him but, the sin against the Holy Ghost literally, cannot be forgiven. In the book of Mark 3:24 says, " *but he that shall blaspheme against the Holy Ghost hath never forgiveness, but is in danger of eternal damnation.*"In one scenario, in the book of Matthew, Jesus cast devils from the possessed, blind and dumb person but was mocked by the Pharisees which said that he cast out devils but, by Beelzeebub, the prince of the devils, however, Jesus rebuked them in *Matthew 12:30-31* which read, " *He that is not with me is against me, and he that gathereth not with me scattered abroad. Wherefore I say unto you, all manner of sin and blasphemy shall be forgiven unto men. But the blasphemy against the Holy Ghost shall not be forgiven unto men.*"

Jesus himself said, sin against the Holy Ghost is not forgiven. Therefore, it is very clear that sin against the Holy Ghost is literally unforgiven, and no amount of prayers shall not work to save the one who has sinned. The sins that believers keep on doing or repeating can no longer be forgiven. This is testified in *Hebrew 10:26,." If we deliberately keep on sinning after we have received the knowledge of the truth, <u>no sacrifice is left</u>.*" So if a believer keeps repeating the same sins there will be no more sacrifice or no way to be forgiven even if somebody prays for him or if he repents for his sins because chances have been forfeited or lost.

Immortal sin

Immortal sin is the sin that can be forgiven by God that even if we sin against the Son of God, He is ready to forgive us. If a man sins against the Lord Jesus Christ, he can still be forgiven if he wholeheartedly asks for forgiveness. *Matthew 12: 32* says, " *And whosoever speaketh a word against the Son of man, it shall be forgiven him; neither in this world, neither in the world to come.*" Even if the Son of man was mocked during the time when he was on the cross, the mocker could be forgiven. The bible tells how the Son of man was mocked , In *Matthew 27 :42 says " He save others , himself he cannot save. If he be the King of Israel, let him now come down from the cross, and we will believe him.*"

These are the words of one of the thieves who cast insulting words against the Son of Man. What do you think was he forgiven ? The bible says, you may be forgiven if you sin against the Son of Man.

Confession of Sins

To whom shall we confess our sins and inequities? The bible says, confess your transgressions unto the Lord. Let us read, *Psalms 32:5*, " *I acknowledge my sin unto thee, and mine iniquity have I not hid, I said, I will confess my transgressions unto the Lord; and thou forgavest the iniquity of my sin.*" We should not say that we have not sinned. There are times that we do not know that we have offended God or we have committed sins in our daily undertakings. We should confess them all.

Let us read, *1John 1:8-9*,"*If we say that we have no sin, we deceive ourselves, and the truth is not in us. If we confess our sins, he is faithful and just to forgive us our sins, and to cleanse us from all unrighteousness.*" When you sin against your brethren, confess and forgive one another. Let us read, James 5:16 which reads, " *Confess your faults one to another, and pray one for another, that ye may be healed.*"

Shall we clean ourselves from our sins by harming or punishing ourselves in such a way that we feel that it is the best way to be cleansed? No. It is unchristian to punish yourselves by way of whipping you body or walking by your knees. But the more you are committing sin by doing those vain things.

Let us read *Colossians 2:23,* " *which things have indeed a show of wisdom in will worship, and humility, and neglecting of the body; not in any honor to the satisfying of the flesh.*" It means that one cannot repent and compensate the sins he has committed by harming the body as a means of sacrifice just to be forgiven and satisfy the requirement for forgiveness. It is not that way.

Are Sins Transferable to Descendants ?

Are Sins Inheritable and Transferable ?

Many superstitious and non- bible reading people say that sin of a man is inheritable from birth because the first humans Adam and Eve sinned before the Lord God. In this situation enlightened Christians can firmly rebut this allegation that sin is inheritable and transferable to kin.

How can an infant or new-born child sin if he or she does not know anything in this world? Can you blatantly accuse an innocent person of an offense he has not done? Apparently, unfair and inequitable because it is bad to punish an innocent person. To prove that we really do not inherit sins of parents, let us read *Matthew 1'2:41,* " *Jesus said, let the little children come to me, and do not for the kingdom of heaven belongs to such as these.*" The verse says that kingdom of heaven belongs to the little children. How can such little children commit sin ? This also implies that children or babies are assured of salvation because Christ said the kingdom of heaven belongs to little children. Sin is only committed by persons who can already discern what is right and wrong. What does sin mean ?

The bible will answer the meaning of sin. In *1 John 3:4* reads , " *Everyone who sins breaks the law, in fact, sin is lawlessness*". It is defined as lawlessness. Men commit sin intentionally or unintentionally. Sins or transgressions of men are punishable in due time. Did you know that you committed sin if you knew what was right and you did not do it? This is what the law says in *James 4:17* which says, " *Anyone, then, who knows the good he ought to do and doesn't do it, sins.*" Another verse proves that little children do not sin is found in *Hebrew* 5:13, " *Anyone who lives in milk, being an infant is not acquainted with the teaching about righteousness.*" Conclusively, we can't reason out that sin is inherited from birth. This verse tells that something is inherited and not a sin. *Proverbs 19:14* reads, " *Houses and wealth are inherited from parents, but a prudent wife is from the Lord.*"

Furthermore, people know that sons of men will not inherit nor share with the Father's sin. This explains that sin is not inherited by children. This is testified in *Ezekiel 18:20*, " *The souls who sin is the one who will die. The son will not share the guilt of the father, nor ;will the father share the guilt of the son.*" Perhaps you may ask, How about the law of God in *Exodus 20:4-5* which read, " *that children of the third and fourth generations because of the sins of their father*?" This is one of the Ten Commandments given to Moses for the people of Israel, and not for the Gentiles. Although that commandment is appropriate to the Gentiles, even nowadays, *Exodus 20:5* is not applicable to Christians. This is because this law has been changed.

The proof that can be read in Hebrew 14:33 which reads, " *for when there is a change of the priesthood, there must also be a change of the law.*" In fact men are the ones creating his own sins. Read this in *Proverbs 16*: , " *In his heart a man plans his course, but the Lord determines his steps.*"

Note: The aforementioned laws are only applicable to the Christian members of the Church of God that are written and taught in the bible.

Apostles and Prophets Also Sin

Who among the servants in the bible sinned?

Like Angels that sin , Prophets and Apostles were human beings who were given free will also to choose which is right and wrong on earth. Therefore, they also sinned. Moses, was a prophet and deliverer sent by God together with Aaron and Miriam to free their people from the bondage of Egypt. Aaron and Miriam sinned when they criticized Moses of marrying an Ethiopian woman. They talked against Moses and God heard them. This scenario can be read in Numbers 12:1-2, " And Miriam and Aaron spake against Moses because of the Ethiopian woman whom he had married: for he had married an Ethiopian woman. And they said, Hath the Lord heard it."

On the other hand, Moses sinned when he disobeyed God. They were not able to enter the promise land, but only Caleb and Joshua. Moses was not able to enter, too. Let us read, Numbers 14:30 " doubtless ye shall not come into the land, concerning which I swear to make you dwell therein, save Caleb the son of Jephun'neh, and Joshua the son of Nun.Abraham also sinned for disobedience. He heeded Sarah's request to sleep with their house servant, Hagar, which Abram did and they bore a son, Ishmael. God did not want him do that and yet did not wait for the command and will . Let us read Genesis 20:6-7, " And God said unto him in a dream, Yea, I know that thou didst this in the integrity of thy heart; for I also withheld thee from sinning against me; therefore suffered I thee not to touch her. Now, therefore restore the man his wife; for he is a prophet, and he shall pray for thee, and thou shalt live; and if thou shalt surely die, thou, and all that are thine."

Let us read Genesis 16:1-4, " Now Sarai, Abram's wife, bare him no children: and she had a handmaid, an Egyptian, whose name was Hagar. And Sarai said unto Abram, Behold now, the Lord hath restrained me from bearing: I pray thee, go in unto my maid; it may be that I may obtain children by her. And Abram hearkened to the voice of Sarai. And Sarai, Abram's wife, took Hagar her maid the Egyptian, after Abram had dwelt ten years in the land of Canaan, and gave her to her husband Abram to be his wife. And he went in unto Hagar, and she conceived: and when she saw that she had conceived: her mistress was despised in her eyes."

Abraham did not wait God's promise that he would be made a father of many nations. In the New Testament, the apostles and disciples of our Lord Jesus Christ also sinned when they went home to their respective homes without fully-knowing the truth written in the bible of the promised resurrection of the Christ on the third day. They ignored the knowledge from Christ about the resurrection and instead went their way home.

The vigil and waiting were in vain when they did not wait but instead went home without knowing the fact of the resurrection of Christ. The fact can be read in John 20:9-10, " For as yet they knew not the Scripture, that he must rise again from the dead. Then the disciples went away again unto their own home." The disciples did not know the importance of the teachings they should have known that time. The Apostle Peter sinned when he disobeyed the Lord's command in Acts 10:9-16. " On the morrow, as they went on their journey; and drew nigh unto the city, Peter went up upon the housetop to pray about the sixth hour; and he became very hungry, and would have eaten; but while they made ready, he fell into a trance, and saw heaven opened, and a certain vessel descending unto him, as it had been a great sheet knit at the four corners, and let down to the earth: wherein were all manner of four-footed beasts of the earth, and wild beasts, and creeping things, and fowls of the air,, And there came a voice to him, "Rise, Peter; kill, and eat."

But Peter said, Not so, Lord; for I have never eaten anything that is common or unclean. And the voice spake unto him again the second time. What God hath cleansed, that call not thou common, This was done thrice, and the vessel was received up again into heaven."Peter and all the disciples sinned when they denied the Lord. Let us read Matthew 26:34-35 ' Jesus said unto him, Verily I say unto thee, That his night, before the cock crow, thou shalt deny me thrice. Peter said unto him, Though I should die with thee, yet will I not deny thee. Likewise also said all the disciples."During that time the chosen people (Israelites) were forbidden to dine with the Gentiles as it was considered a grave sin for them. However, the question is, did Peter eat with the Gentiles? Yes, that is why when he went to Antioch he was rebuked by the Apostle Paul. Let us read Galacia 2:11-14 " But when Peter was come to Antioch, I withstood him to the face, because he was to be blamed.

For before that certain came from James, he did eat with the Gentiles; but when they were come, he withdrew and separated himself, fearing them which were of the circumcision. And the other Jews dissembled, likewise with him; insomuch that Barnabas also was carried away with their dissimulation.

But when I saw that they walked not uprightly according to the truth of the gospel, I said unto Peter before them all, If thou, being a Jew, livest after the manner of Gentiles, and not as do the Jews, why compellest thou the Gentiles to live as do the Jews? The Apostle Philip also sinned when he asked our Lord Jesus Christ impertinent question, requesting Him to show the Father for them. Let us read John 14: 8 " Philip saith unto him, Lord, show us the Father, and it sufficieth us." The request of Philip is ignorance of the teaching and showed impertinency because nobody has seen the Father. Let us read, John 4:24 " God is a Spirit; and they that worship him must worship him in spirit and in truth," And because God is a spirit, nobody can see Him and it is impossible for those who see to live".

Let us read Exodus 33:20 " And he said, Thou canst not see my face; for there shall no man see me, and live."It is only the Son of God who is with Him that see him face to face. Therefore, Philip was at fault when he asked that request of the Lord for he did not understand what he was saying."Therefore, all men on earth have sinned and nobody lives without sinning except our Lord Jesus Christ and the infants. Let us read Romans 3:23 "for all have sinned, and come short of the glory of God."

Transgressions of Angels

What kind of transgressions did angels commit? Angels crossed-bred with human beings and begotten abnormally grown siblings (giants). They sowed wickedness and continued to sin. Let us read Genesis 6:4-5, " There were giants in the earth in those days; and also after that, when the sons of God came in unto the daughters of men, and they bare children to them, the same became mighty men which were of old, men of renown." And God saw that the wickedness of man was great in the earth, and that every imagination of the thoughts of his heart was only evil continually."

The angels that were assigned to do their tasks left their habitation or post. Let us read Jude 1:6, " And the angels which kept not their first estate, <u>but left their own habitation</u>, he hath reserved in everlasting chains under darkness unto the judgment of the great day." Note that these angels were made perfect in spirit but eventually became perfect in flesh. Meaning they did the work of the flesh. Let us read Galatians 3:3, " Are ye so foolish? Having begun in the Spirit, are ye now made perfect by the flesh?"

While angels have committed sins in the past, the question is: Will they(angels) commit sins again ? Yes. Let us read Revelation 22:8-9, " And I John saw these things, and heard them. And when I had heard and seen, I fell down to worship before the feet of the angel which showed me these things. Then saith he unto me, See thou do it not: for I am thy fellow servant, and of thy brethren the prophets, and of them which keep the sayings of this book: worship God." These verses prove that angels are like human beings also who could sin again because judgment has not yet come. They are also created to serve God like human beings waiting for the last day of judgment. They will also be subjected to be judged as what we have discussed in earlier discussion.

Christians Will Judge the Sinning Angels

Would you believe that Saints (referring to Christians) shall judge the angels in the last day? In the last day or judgment day, Christians would not be the only ones to be judged but also the sinning angels who were commissioned to do certain tasks by God would be judged by Christians. What is surprising is that these celestial beings whom we normally thought of being saved already in heavens would be judged by Christian-saints and those condemned would be thrown to hell. Let us read I Corinthians 6:2-3 " Do ye not know that the saints shall judge the smallest matters? Know ye not that we shall judge angels? How much more things that pertain to this life?"

Angels sin because they are also given free will to do right and wrong, however, they are accountable to their actions although angels know all things on earth and so powerful spirit beings . However, not all of them are given the right to know more things beyond what has been given them by God. Does God trust all angels? Not all angels are trusted nor entrusted with the knowledge of the mystery in heaven neither are they superior to the Son of God (Lord Jesus Christ). This is asserted in Job4:18, " Behold, he put no trust in his servants; and his angels he charged with folly;"

Neither the angels were told about the Sonship of Lord Jesus Christ. Let us read, Hebrew 1:5, " For unto which of the angels said he at any time, Thou art my Son, this day have I begotten thee? And again, I will be to him a Father, and he shall be to me a Son?" Therefore, as angels are prone to sin like Christians they would be judged in the last days and thrown into hell. Let us read II Peter 2:4, " For if God spared not the angels that sinned, but cast them down to hell," and delivered them into chains" of darkness, to be reserved unto judgment."

The Death Of A Sinning Soul

The bible states in Ezekiel 18:4, " The soul that is sinning –it itself will die." The prophet Elijah began to ask that his soul might die (1Kings 19:4) Likewise Jonah kept asking that his soul might die."(Jonah 4:8). The soul dies when a person dies because we are mortal beings. Since a person is a soul when he dies, his soul which is a physical being dies. Concerning what happened to Rachel when she gave birth to a son, the bible in Genesis 35:18 says: As her soul was going out she called his name Ben-oni; but his father called him Benjamin."

And referring to the resurrection of a widow's son, in 1Kings 17:22 states: " God listened to Elijah's voice, so that the soul of the child came back within him and he came to life." The life that returned to the boy was the spirit that is life. Life means spirit that is in our nostrils so we can breathe.

To further our knowledge about this study, we should know the compositions of man. Man contains three elements: The spirit, soul and body. Let us read I Thessalonians 5:23," May God himself the God of peace, sanctify you through and through. May your whole spirit, soul and body be kept blameless at the coming of Jesus Christ." The bible also tells us that there is what is called inner man which is the spirit. The inner is renewed upon baptism after receiving and believing the doctrine of our Lord Jesus Christ. The old inner man (spirit) is renewed or replaced with a new inner man which worships God.

Notice nowadays, that there are false teachings about Christianity The bible tells us of the emergence of the false prophets in later times. Let us read the proof in Romans 14:33, " for such people are not serving our Lord Christ, but their own appetites. By smooth talk and flattery they deceive the minds of native people." People should beware of these kinds of disguised servants of the Lord, otherwise your souls will be in danger. In this instance, if you have been listening to uncertain teachings while you have been abiding by what you have been taught of as you are already doing things outside the biblical standards, you ought to examine and search yourselves if you are still in the right track.

The bible tell us in 2Corinthians 13:5, " Examine yourselves to see whether you are in the faith.". Therefore, the verse tells us to test yourselves. Do you realize that Christ Jesus is in you unless of course, you fail the test. We are told by this verse to examine ourselves if we are still in the faith. Are you still in the faith? Or you have been repudiated by Christ ? See yourselves if you are still in the faith.

Nowadays we are living a dangerous time. Many men are wicked and merciless. These are the times when men are living dangerously as may be compared in the past. Criminality is rampant. Notice the changes in the society of men now. What do you observe in your environment and in the news around the globe. What is now common ? You can really never trust a stranger nor any men. Illegal drugs cause many men to commit crime and suicide. Poverty causes man to die, likewise suicide and commission of crime happen most of the time. Many things could happen in many places in most unexpected time.

The bible tells us in Romans 3:10, As it is written: " There is no one righteous, not even one. " Despite this assertion the bible tells us that there are still perfect men in the past and in the present time. No one was found righteous on that particular place, but the bible reveals there are places also where righteous men dwelt. Let us read, Job 1:1, " In the land of Uz there lived a man whose name was Job. This man was blameless and upright, he feared God and shunned evil."

CHAPTER 8

Salvation and Religion

The bible says, Seek ye first the Kingdom of God and all these things shall be added unto you. We do not live by bread alone, but in every word that comes from Him. There may be many churches nowadays as there are many kinds of believers that still believe in the motto, God first before anything else . There are those who are already under the law who do the law and others who are under the law but do not do the law, and there are those who are not under the law but they do the law of God and Christ. While the unbelievers say, "there is no God", the bible calls them "fools". Life does not end on earth but after death there will be one day judgment to wait and the dead will rest for the meantime and rise together with the living in the last day. The popular quotation, " To die is to rest", may mean physical freedom and escape from this turbulent world.

When we die our dead body returns to dust while the spirit goes back to the Maker who holds every breath of life on earth. But in the last day, the resting dead will rise from their lengthy slumber and together with the living everyone will face the Great White throne judgment. A judgment where there is no more slumber and rest, but eternal torment to those who deserve to be cast into the lake of burning sulfur and brimstone and everlasting life to those who will be saved. To elaborate further, the bible says,"

For it is destined unto men to die once and after that the judgment." It means that man will die first, but not to be judged right away for glory or condemnation. His flesh will return to dust as his spirit returns to God. When Christ returns to earth there will be resurrection of the dead in Christ first. He will reign a thousand years to give chance to those who have not received Christ nor given up their evil works. After a thousand years have elapsed, the second resurrection will occur and after that, everyone will face the Judgment Throne of God.

And there, each one of us will be judged according to the record in the book of life. At that point in time, everyone will face his fate whether in the glory of heaven or into the excruciating pain of the lake of fire, that is the so-called, second death. This spiritual death is not literal as in total extinction from reality of the torment of punishment. But to physically suffer the torment of fire. The condemned will not be in the spirit but they will be revived in the flesh as if they were in the natural world in order to receive the punishment that they deserve. The bible says, they will suffer the torment in hell day and night.

When we speak of spiritual issues and religion we speak of our soul's salvation and our destiny in the life after death. And we should realize that everything on earth is temporal since earth is the testing ground for mankind and the results of our activities here are all recorded in each own book in heaven where men will be judged accordingly. Our lives may always be focused on what we see (material things) on earth but the reality is , there are unseen things that are coming along the way.

Those unseen things have something to do with each own faith. It is very crucial that while we are still on earth we make sure that our spiritual and religious beliefs are guided by the truth in the bible (good for Christians) which is the word of God. It is the truth that our Lord Jesus Christ and his disciples are teaching then and now.

Most probably, the Word has reached many nations now with the help of modern technology as compared in the past. The bible says that the gospel will be preached to all nations of the world and it has been made possible by this modern technology today as it is told in the bible, this is one prophecy that has been fulfilled.

In this present Christian dispensation, the original teachings of the Christ and the disciples have been restored and found now, since the book (bible) had been sealed for many centuries as what the bible tells in *Daniel 12: 4* that says, *"But thou, O Daniel, shut up the words, and seal the book, even to the time of the end:"* For many centuries, the mystery of the bible had been sealed even if the pages had been browsed and read by many groups and individuals who were trying to interpret the words .

The fact is, it is given only to the people of God in this end time generation to understand and prophesy the words. The mystery to know the words in the bible is only given to the chosen people of God as it is written in Mark 4:11, *" And he said unto them, Unto you it is given to know the mystery of the kingdom of God; but unto them that are without, all these things are done in parables:"* The mystery of the kingdom of God in the verse refers to God's "Word".In this bible verse, it is clearly pronounced that the mystery of the word to know is given only to appointed ones but to those without it will be done in parables.

In other words, those groups who did not received the mystery to know would not be able to know it but they would just read the word plainly or literally as it is, unless they cleave to which is right and good in the bible (i.e., to believe and obey the law and doctrine of the Lord Jesus Christ) and be baptized as they walk in it for the rest of their lives. In the last days, many will be purified as many will continue to become wicked and the old path which is the former teachings of God will be understood and taught to all, that is already happening today. Remember that the basis of our salvation is the teachings of God and Lord Jesus Christ in the bible which tell mankind that the gospel is the power of God to salvation.

According to the Apostle, Paul in *Romans 1:16, ". For I am not ashamed of the gospel of Christ; for it is the power of God unto salvation to everyone that believeth; to the Jew first, and also to the Greek."*Speaking of religion, your salvation relies heavily on what your preacher or pastor teaches you about faith and salvation.

Remember that Salvation is not taken in an instant pronouncement of any one or by your own pronouncement that you receive Christ as your personal Lord and Savior as what your brethren-leader may ask you to do. Salvation is a process.

It will be discussed in this book later. Everyone should know that church leaders have the most responsibility and accountability for your salvation. The bible tells that if you are led and taught a wrong religious doctrine and embrace them, you and your leader will be in danger of being condemned into the lake of fire in the judgment day. The bible says in the book of *Matthew, 15:14, " Let them alone; they be blind leaders of the blind. And if the blind lead the blind, both shall fall into the ditch."* When you find that you are in the wrong faith or church it is very important that you come out of her or you will be stained of her guilt and share the punishment intended for her.

The bible says, " Come out of her" , you may be partakers of her sins and the plagues that shall be scourged upon her iniquities, says the Lord. Revelation 18:4 says, And I heard another voice from heaven, saying, come out of her, my people, that ye be not partakers of her sins, and that ye receive not of her plagues," While there is still time, people are being commanded to come out of her so that they will not partake from her sins and punishment in the judgment day.

The verse gives emphasis to the pronoun " her" because it is the gender that is being referred to the church. In the book of Revelation, the church is referred to "Babylon" or congregations of persons as the pronoun used is "her". The bible commands us to cleave to that which is good (Romans 12:9)in order to know the truth and be partakers of the good things from God and His Son. Many believe that after dying everything is over According to their beliefs they would go to heaven, if not, to hell or purgatory.

Some believe that after dying man will be reincarnated into another form of creatures such as animal, plants and other objects. Some fundamentalists who read the bible think that life does not end after departing earth. They have come to believe that there is an event that would happen in the future. They may even ask themselves these questions : Where are we heading from here? Shall we go to eternal life or life in hell? Remember that your soul and salvation are at stake when you cleave to a particular religious belief.

Because when you entrust your soul to a wrong belief and teachings about Christ's doctrine , you will not be able to redeem it when you are already dead. Therefore, when you have found the true teachings, leave the wrong teachings and cleave to that which is good that you may be saved in the last day like what the Apostle Paul did when he left his belief in Judaism and cleaved to the teachings of Christ in the Church of God which already exists today. But the problem is, there are many churches of God today and you may not be able to know which is which.

Many false teachings appear into world today teaching and confessing about God and Jesus Christ. People will be confused which of these congregations is telling truth. The bible ascertains us that you will be able to determine the true church and cleave with them. The bible teaches us in 1 John 4:1, "test every spirit if it is of God". You are free to search the truth. Try to hear them and determine whether they are of God. Don't stop searching who among these teachers is telling truth. Study and consult the bible. The Lord God will guide you to the real one. What is that eternal and everlasting life.? Everyone on earth should realize that life does not end on earth but a time will come when everyone will rise to life everlasting and others to hell.

Once you have read , heard and listened and ultimately believed, do not hesitate, do not delay, and that once you believe that it is true and good, do it , be baptized (*Matthew 28:19-20,"Go ye therefore, and teach all nations, baptizing them in the name of the Father,and of the Son, and of the Holy Ghost; teaching them to observe all things whatsoever I have commanded you, and lo, I am with you always, even unto the end of the world. Amen")* because when you lose it you lose your chance of being saved. Save yourself...in the last day. (*Ezekiel 14:20, " though Noah, Daniel and Job, we in it, as I live, saith the Lord GOD, they shall deliver neither son nor daughter; they shall but deliver their own souls by their righteousness.*"You alone will be the one to save yourself and no other person can save you when judgment comes.

You will do it according to the bible. Beware of the teachers of faith. You must see to it that you are not misled because there are many false prophets or spiritual teachers nowadays.

Be sure that every spiritual statement that they pronounce to you is founded in the bible or supported by scriptural verses and that they are truly existing and happening, otherwise, they are fallacious pronouncements that should be accursed! According to the bible's instructions if any man or angel shall preach the doctrine that is different from the doctrine of Christ accursed him! *Galatians 1:8, " But though we, or an angel from heaven, preach any other gospel unto you than that which we have preached unto you, let him be accursed."*

See to it that spiritual statements are biblically founded because only the bible must be the source of every pronouncement that church leaders should cite when teaching. It must be affirmed by all Christians that the teachings of Christ is the key to salvation and not by mere accepting Him as Lord and Savior. How can you be saved if you don't know his instructions and teachings. How will you do His will and commandments without knowing it ? *1 Corinthians 15:1-2 say, "Moreover, brethren, I declare unto you the gospel which I preached unto you, which also ye have received, and wherein ye stand, by which also ye are saved, if ye keep in memory what I preached unto you, unless ye have believed in vain."*

But, we should realize that the bible teaches us that those who do not want the Word (law) or teachings will be condemned in the last day. *Romans 2:11-15, "for there is no respect of persons with God. For as many as have <u>sinned without law shall also perish without law</u>; and* *as many as have sinned in the law shall be judged by the law."*In other words, by knowing the true teachings in the bible shall we be able to know about salvation

Steps Of Salvation

How can we be saved in the last day? Life does not end after dying. There is life after death, and this is proven by the bible as we have already known. The question is how can you attain salvation in order to be saved when judgment day comes. Is it by just accepting Jesus Christ as Lord and Savior and then you are already saved? Do not be misled by this notion because Salvation is a process and not an instant act. Salvation is believing the Word of God. When you hear the Word and believe in your heart after proving it in the bible then accept it. The bible in 1 *John 4:1,* reads, "*Beloved, believe not every spirit, but try the spirits whether they are of God; because many false prophets are gone out into the world.*" When you have proven and tested that it is the teachings of Christ, believe it in your heart. Let us read, *Acts 16:31*, "*If you believe you have the right teachings then you believe it. You will now be baptized for the cleansing of your sins.*

Let us read Acts 22:16, "And now why tarriest thou? Arise, and be baptized, and wash away thy sins, calling on the name of the Lord."

When you have been baptized you are converted into a Christian and you should be called Christian in your faith. Let us read *Acts 11:26*, " *and when he had found him, he brought him unto Antioch. And it came to pass, that a whole year they assembled themselves with the church, and taught much people. And the disciples were called Christians first in Antioch.*" This verse proves that true believers in Christ are called Christians. When you received baptism you become a new creation.

Let us read, *Romans 6:4,6,7* which read,: *Therefore we are buried with him by baptism into death: that like as Christ was raised up from the dead by the glory of the Father, even so we also should walk in newness of life." knowing this, that our old man is crucified with him, that the body of sin might be destroyed, that henceforth we should not serve sin. For he that is dead is freed from sin."* When you have received the true teachings you will work for it and take care of what you have received as instructed in *1Corinthians 15:1-2* which read, "*Moreover, brethren, I declare unto you the gospel which I preached unto you, which also ye have received, and wherein ye stand; by which also ye are saved, if ye keep in memory what I preached unto you, unless ye have believed in vain.*"

Remember that Salvation is not that easily attained. You will persevere and live according to the will of God until the end. Let us read *Matthew 10:22*, "*And ye shall be hated of all men for my name's sake, but he that endureth to the end shall be saved.*" This verse proves that salvation is a long suffering.

When you become a follower and disciple of Christ, and as you live a Christian living observing and *obeying the laws you are tasked also to teach others as instructed in Matthew 28:19" Go ye therefore, and teach all nations, baptizing them in the name of the Father, and of the Son, and of the Holy Ghost;" teaching them to observe all things whatsoever I have commanded you; and lo, I am with you always, even unto the end of the world, Amen.*" You should realize that all these things will not end in vain because you will certainly be saved when that day comes.

Remember that there is tribulation on earth and believers are always experiencing tribulation but they are not alone. Where there is tribulation there is strength that Christians will experience to overcome their problems. This is an assurance that you are a Christian destined to walk to the right path.

However, your salvation must not be entrusted to any person or to any religious authority because you alone will work out for your own salvation. This is what the bible is telling us *in Ezekiel 14:20*, "*though Noah, Daniel and Job, were in it, as I live, saith the Lord*

GOD, they shall deliver neither son nor daughter; they shall but deliver own souls by their righteousness."

Knowledge of Salvation

What are the ways to be saved before the last day comes? As stated previously, we continue with the Word in the bible because it is the source of knowledge by which we shall know what to do and how we are going to obey God. Let us read, *I Corinthians 15:1-2.* " *Moreover, brethren, I declare unto you the gospel which I preached unto you the gospel which also ye have received and wherein ye stand; by which also are saved, if ye keep in memory what I preached unto you, unless ye have believed in vain."*

In this verse Paul is telling the believers that the gospel where he got his preaching should be kept in memory by which we can be saved. In another verse he also affirmed that the gospel is the power of God to salvation. In *Romans 1:16,* " *For I am not ashamed of the gospel of Christ; for it is the power of God unto salvation to everyone that believeth; to the Jew first, and also to the Greek."*

Therefore, the gospel is one way to be saved. In the near end many things will happen as that day draws nearer. As we have already tackled about the signs of times, another sign is that many will be cleansed and purified meaning many will try to find the truth in the bible for understanding but those wicked whose purpose is awkward will never find them even if they read the bible.

Many will travel to and fro because of advanced and modern transportation that men have invented and built, and knowledge will increase. Let us read, Daniel 12:4 "But thou, O Daniel, shut up the words, and seal the book, even to the time of the end; many shall run to and fro, and knowledge shall be increased. Take note that being a baptized-Christian you walk by faith to a new path to maintain your salvation. You must be aware and realized that there is tribulation to those who follow the walks of Christ.

Expect all sufferings of being a Christian as the bible says in *Mateo 24:9, " Then shall they deliver you up to be afflicted, and shall kill you; and ye shall be hatred of all nations for my name's sake."* You should also realize that a Christian who has become a disciple will experience the reality of tests. Do not be surprised that a Christian shall experience hatred and he may even be left lonely by the world. *Matthew 10:22," And ye shall be hated of all men for my name's sake; but he that endureth to the end shall be saved*" But the price to those who endure these sufferings shall be salvation.

Do not be surprised also that in the midst of a Christian's tribulation he will be hated by your very own family. *Matthew 10:36 " And a man's foes shall be his household."* But He promised that despite man's tribulation he will have peace in Christ because since He has overcome the world His disciples will also overcome it with cheer. *John 16:33, says " These things I have spoken unto you, that in me ye might have peace. In the world ye shall have tribulation, but be of good cheer; I have overcome the world."*

Therefore, being a Christian is not that easy especially to those newly-baptized Christian converts. They will pass through the test of fire. A process that will purify them like gold in order to edify their Christian-faith. Can salvation be forfeited or lost? It is not true that when you have become a believer you will forever be saved. As discussed it is not easy to be saved. It is a process until the end. Salvation can be forfeited or lost. You have to take care of it. Let us read *II Corinthians 13:5, " Examine yourselves, whether ye not your own faith; prove your own selves; know ye not your own selves, how that Jesus Christ is in you, except ye be reprobates?"*

Therefore, Christians in the long run should take care of what they have received because there is danger in neglecting your salvation. It doesn't mean you can do anything you want to do because you have been saved. You must keep the teachings of God and obey them. It is difficult to live a Christian way but it is a key to salvation. We must do good and keep His word. According to the bible.

Those who will persevere in this world will be saved in the last day. Therefore, as parting word Brethren, while there is still time seek the Lord and find His will so that you may also be saved on that day. That day is near. The Lord has been instructing us to ask our pastor, minister, church-head, evangelist or teacher of faith concerning the genuine teachings of Christ and biblical issues pertaining to salvation .

Let us read *Haggai 2:11* which reads, " *Thus saith the LORD of hosts; Ask now the priests concerning the law, saying..*" It is necessary to know things from the bible and ask our church leaders if they know what they are teaching. You can prove if they are of God by asking issues about the laws of God. This is one way by which you may not be deceived because false prophets are out to deceive people, otherwise you and your leader will go down to the pit of death as the bible tells and in the same way it was told us to be wise in this world particularly at this point when we are living a dangerous time.

Therefore, if you are a Christian work out your salvation with fear and trembling as what the bible teaches in *Philippians 2:12* say, " *Wherefore, my beloved, as ye have always obeyed, not as in my presence only, but now much more in my presence only, but now much more in my absence, work out your own salvation with fear and trembling.*"

Path to Salvation

In *II Timothy 2:22* reads," *Flee also youthful lusts; but follow righteousness, faith, charity, peace, with them that call on the Lord out of pure heart.*" If we maintain our heart's inequities we will suffer the consequence of it. The book of *Isaiah 59:11* says, " *we look for judgment, but there is none, for salvation, but it is far off from us.*". Therefore, salvation for people whose hearts are filthy is far and cannot be found.

This is what *I Thessalonians 4: 1-5* read, " *Furthermore then we beseech you, brethren, and exhort you by the Lord Jesus, that as ye have received of us how ye ought to walk and to please God, so ye would abound more and more. For ye know what commandments we gave you by the Lord Jesus. For this is the will of God, even your sanctification, that ye should abstain from fornication: that every one of you should know how to possess his vessel in sanctification and honor: not in the lust of concupiscence, even as the Gentiles which know not God:*"

A life that is pleasing is a life that is according to the will of God in the bible. Live a holy life as the bible instructs believers. A verse in the book of Luke says, " *And he said to them all, If any man will come after me, let him deny himself, and take up his cross daily, and follow me.*" No man can say he is free of sin. According to the bible, " All have sinned and come short to the glory of God." Therefore, if all have sinned we can be free from being sinners. *I John 1:8-9* say, " *If we say that we have no sin, we deceive ourselves, and the truth is not in us. If we confess our sins, he is faithful and just to forgive us our sins, and to cleanse us from all unrighteousness. If we say that we have not sinned, we make him a liar, and his word is not in us.*"

Therefore, we can only be cleansed of our sins when we confess them to God. And God will forgive you of your inequity, hence, you leave your old self and sin no more . *Psalms 32:5*, says, " *I acknowledged my sin unto thee, and mine iniquity have I not hid. I said, I will confess my transgressions unto the Lord; and thou forgavest the iniquity of my sin.*"

If you are forgiven, then you should not go back to your old self as you do because if you commit the same sins repetitively, you will not be forgiven anymore, however, you should avoid sinning while you sin willfully. If we keep on doing the same sins, then we shall not be forgiven anymore. This is proven in *Hebrew 10:26.* " *For if we sin willfully after that we have received the knowledge of the truth, there remaineth no more sacrifice for sins.*"

Forfeiture of Salvation of Christians

Some Christian-professed leaders teach their members that once they have become Christians or converts they are already saved all the days of their lives. They did not know that salvation can be lost if they have neglected it . This is what *2 Corinthians 13:5 says, " Examine yourselves, whether ye be in the faith; prove your own selves. Know ye not your own selves, how that Jesus Christ is in you, except ye be reprobates?"*

A Christian who is proven to have lost his belief and goes astray may find himself repudiated by our Lord Jesus Christ. In other words, a Christian can lose his salvation after neglecting what he or she has received. We should realize that salvation is not only accepting our Lord Jesus Christ but we must realize that accepting His teachings is accepting our Lord Jesus Christ. When we listen and believe in His teachings and baptized we receive a new Spirit and we walk in a new life. We should always keep in mind, (*1 Corinthians 15:1-2, " Moreover, brethren, I declare unto you the gospel which I preached unto you, which also ye have received, and wherein ye stand; by which also ye are saved, if ye keep in memory what I preached unto you, unless ye have believed in vain.")* hearts and action the teachings of Christ, but if we neglect the teachings and continue in wicked ways, salvation is lost.

Hebrew 6:4-6 say, " *For it is impossible for those who were once enlightened, and have tasted of the heavenly gift, and were made partakers of the Holy Ghost, and have tasted the good word of God, and the powers of the world to come, if they shall fall away, to renew them again unto repentance; seeing they crucify to themselves the Son of God afresh, and put him to an open shame."* Those who have found themselves to have lost the salvation and turned away from their faith as back sliders do, they have crucified the Son of God anew.

How can we say then that those who are saved are always saved. We cannot always justify their repetitious sins as excuse for being

Christians who have become children of God before. No. because a Christian who commits sin unintentionally may have a chance to be forgiven and saved but those who repetitiously commit sins intentionally will not be have a chance to be forgiven and saved.

The bible say in James 1:14-15, " but every man is tempted, when he is drawn away of his own lust, and enticed. Then when lust hath conceived, it bringeth forth sin; and sin, when it is finished, bringeth forth death." If you let yourself tempted to the lust of sin it may bring you death. The bible says, there is no more sacrifice left for them which means, they cannot be forgiven anymore. *Hebrew 10:26-27 " For it we sin willfully after that we have received the knowledge of the truth, there remaineth no more sacrifice for sins."*Many Christians interpret that salvation in scriptural verse in *Ephesians 2:8-9," For by grace are ye saved through faith; and that not of yourselves: it is the gift of God: not of works, lest any man should boast.",* is attained without works anymore but mere faith alone is enough in order for one to be saved.

That is not correct because without works we cannot be saved as *Philippians 2:12 says," Wherefore, my beloved, as ye have always obeyed, not as in my presence only, but now much more in my absence, work out your own salvation with fear and trembling."*

This is very clear, salvation must be worked out with fear and trembling. There are two laws involved Ephesians 2:8-9. The laws of Moses and laws of faith in Christ. In the past, of course, people of God repented and did good works by sacrificing in order to be saved, but in Christian era, we live by faith with works also in Christ Jesus in order to be saved. The question now in the said verses of the book of the Ephesians is, which law are we justified? In *Romans 3:28, " Therefore we conclude that a man is justified by faith without the deeds of the law." . Acts 13:39, says, " and by him all that believe are justified from all things, from which ye could not be justified by the law of Moses."*

Therefore, in this Christian dispensation we are no longer justified under the law of Moses by doing those things that they did before.

We, Christians now have to live and be saved by faith with works in Christ. The phrase, "so that no one could boast" refers to works which man is capable of working in order to be justified for salvation.

These works of salvation that we should do is instructed in 2 Peter 1:3-9, " According to his divine power hath given unto us all things that pertain unto life and godliness, through the knowledge of him that hath called us to glory and virtue; whereby are given unto us exceeding great and precious promises; that by these ye might be partakers of the divine nature, having escaped the corruption that is in the world through lust. And besides this, giving all diligence, add to your faith virtue; and to virtue, knowledge; and to knowledge, temperance; and to temperance, patience; and to patience, godliness; and to godliness, brotherly kindness; and to brotherly kindness, charity.

For if these things be in you, and abound, they make you that ye shall neither be barren nor unfruitful in the knowledge of our Lord Jesus Christ."Remember in the book of the Ephesians in 2:8-9, there are two laws involved: the law of Moses and the law of faith in Christ in which the latter law shall govern all Christians.

Seeking God To Be Saved

When a man lives by himself alone and does not know God, he walks in his own way. Anybody does not know what lies ahead or what is going to happen. It may be happiness, sorrow or death. In this world, many continue in their ways: eating, drinking, marrying, buying and selling and going somewhere else as they wish. James 14:13-14, " *Go to now, ye that say, Today or tomorrow we will go in to such a city, and continue there a year, and buy and sell, and get gain: whereas, ye know not what shall be on tomorrow. For what is your life? It is even a vapor. That appeareth for a little time, and then vanisheth away.*" And because men do not know God's word and even though they have heard about the gospel of Christ they do not listen and instead go their own ways. Worldly men do not find time for spiritual things. The book of Ephesians 4:20-22 read, " *But ye have not so learned Christ ; if so be that ye have heard him, and have been taught by him, as the truth is in Jesus that ye put off concerning the former conversation the old man, which is corrupt according to the deceitful lusts.*"

It is necessary that when the gospel is preached by any pastors, and church-workers, Christians may listen and test the spirit if it is of God because there are many false prophets wandering or out of this world now are preaching about Jesus. 1John 4:1 says, " *Beloved, believe not every Spirit, but try the spirits whether they are of God; because many false prophets are gone out into this world.*" So be very careful and watchful accepting the teachings of these self-professed preachers of faith because you may not know that you are being led to damnation.

There are many false prophets now, test their doctrines if they are really of God. However, the danger is you don't know which is which. By reading and hearing the Word and comparing each doctrine based from the bible, you will be able to test which is true. First, ask God for guidance that you be able to perceive and understand the truth. Be vigilant therefore, that you are not misled to the pit of death.

Man may be exhausted physically in all day's work. When you are in Christ your mind is renewed as the former things in this world have gone out as you think of something worthy. Your body follows the dictate of your mind. In the same manner that Christ is the head of the church and we are his body that follows. You may get tired but there is always renewing of the strength because you believe that Christ renews you daily and you can do all things through Him. Things that will permit Him for you to do. Would you believe that there is something in us that does not get old even if we get physically old? It is the Inner being within us or the so called Spirit that keeps us from living. Our spirit never gets old, even if we get tired and it remains the same. But it does not get tired and we feel strong because of that inner being within us.

The book of II Corinthians 4:16 says, "*For which cause we faint not; but though our outward man perish, yet the inward man is renewed day by day.*" Our inward man is always renewed every day to face our daily tasks in this world. As you realize about our inner man, we now believe that the same inner man (spirit) within us will go back to God who gave it to us when we depart from this earth. This is a reality that there is God who is a Life-Giver. Upon knowing this, we should realize that we should fear Him that can destroy our soul and body, and not anybody else in this wide world because He is the Creator. Matthew 10:28 says, " *And fear not them which kill the body, but are not able to kill the soul; but rather fear Him which is able to destroy both soul and body in hell.*"

When you already heard and understood that you have found the right faith and believe in its doctrine in Christ do not hesitate to pursue the faith. Continue reading and hearing the Word. Salvation cannot be entrusted to anybody else in the church because you will be the one to work out your own salvation. While there is still time man should listen, repent and be baptized, for we never know what lies ahead.

God may not hear us when we ask of Him at the time we need him especially in the last day. Proverbs 1:24-30 read, " *Because I have called and ye refused;*

I have stretched out my hand, and no regarded;
but ye have set at nought all my counsel,
and would none of my reproof;
I also will laugh at your calamity;
I will mock when your fear cometh;
and when your desolation ,

and your destruction cometh as a whirlwind;
when distress and anguish cometh upon you.
then shall they call upon me; but I will not answer;
they shall seek me early, but they shall find me;

for that they hated knowledge, and did not choose the fear of the lord;

they would none of my counsel; they despised all my reproof."

Observe that each line and you will realize the fate of those who turned away or ignored his Word when God was calling them. Calling them through his gospel that is being preached today. The worst scenario that will come is the time of distress and sufferings that may come upon men who hated to learn knowledge about his Word. God will not listen to them when that time comes in the same way that men ignored Him when He was calling them. Men should realize that sinful men shall never see light and his ways and walks will always be wicked. That is an abomination unto the Lord. Proverbs 15:9 says, " *The ways of the wicked is an abomination unto the Lord; but he loveth him that followeth after righteousness."*

Therefore, there is no choice because the wrath of the Lord will surely come in its right time, so hear his Word and don't put off tomorrow before it's too late. II Corinthians 6:2 says, " *(For he saith) I have heard thee in a time accepted and in the day of salvation have I succored thee; behold, now is the accepted time; behold now is the day of salvation."*

Ways of Saving Mankind

Now, if saving is the work of the living God, How does He save? Is God who is in heaven will come down to save men? Will He speak to men for salvation? In the book of Hebrews 1:1-2 say," In the past God spoke to our forefathers through the prophets many times in various ways, but in these last days, he has spoken to us by his Son, whom he appointed heir of all things and through whom he made the universe." With whom God spoke to be instrumental for salvation of men? One of them was Moses, the prophet The book of Acts 7:35, reads," This is the same Moses whom they had rejected with the words, who made you ruler and judge? He was sent to be their ruler and deliverer by God Himself, through the angel who appeared to him in the bush.

He led them out of Egypt and did wonders and miraculous signs in Egypt, at the Red Sea and for forty years in the desert. This is that Moses who told the Israelites, God will send you a prophet like me from your own people." Father God did not personally come down from heaven to save men. He sent a ruler or judge who would do the acts of deliverance, and this is no other than Moses. To sum, up the works of salvation we must not by-pass the authority of God the Father as Savior because in the end overall salvation will be by Him.

Our Lord Jesus Christ had done his work of salvation and the promise of His most awaited coming in the end time on earth is another work of salvation. Moses and other prophets in the bible had done their share In the work of salvation. The works of salvation were done by men of God in different times and in various ways. They have become instrumental in the mission of deliverance of mankind.

Chances of Salvation In The Judgment Day

Are those who have not a chance to hear about the gospel of Christ be saved? What does the bible tell about those who are non-believers and not under the law of Christ ? The bible tells us in Romans 2:11-15 which say, " For there is no respect of persons with God. For as many as have sinned without law shall also perish without law; and as many as have sinned in the law shall be judged by the law; (for not the hearers of the law are just before God, but the doers of the law shall be justified. For when the Gentiles, which have not the law, do by nature the things contained in the law, these, having not the law, are a law unto themselves: which show the work of the law written in their hearts, their conscience also bearing witness, and their thoughts the mean while accusing or else excusing one another;)

Therefore, those who have not heard of the gospel of God shall be justified according to their beliefs and law they follow in their conscience and those who are under the law of God shall be justified according to that law. But those who are not under the law but with pure conscience shall have the chance to be saved and those who are under the law but do not do and obey them shall be in danger of losing salvation. All men shall be justified according to what they have done. But if you hear the correct teachings of the gospel of Christ and you do not hear nor take action to listen you are in danger of being saved.

Let us read Proverbs 1:24-26, "Because I have called, and ye refused; I have stretched out my hand, and no man regarded; but ye have set at nought all my counsel, and would none of my reproof: I also will laugh at your calamity; I will mock when your fear cometh; when your fear cometh as desolation, and your destruction cometh as a whirlwind; when distress and anguish cometh upon you, Then shall call upon me, but I will not answer; they shall seek me early, but they shall not find me; for that they hated knowledge, and did not choose the fear of the LORD; they would none of my counsel; they despised all my reproof. Therefore shall they eat of the fruit of their own way, and be filled with their own devices"

So, therefore, anybody is being warned that if you refuse to listen to the knowledge of the Word of God, even though it is being taught today, nor you pretend you don't hear them preached you will find the consequences in these verses mentioned. Are those outside the true Church of God be saved in the last day? Let us see what the bible answers in 1Corinthians 5:13 which reads, " But them that are without God judgeth.

Therefore put away from among yourselves that wicked person." Therefore, God is the One who will judge those who do not believe and outside the true Church of God, and to those who have not heard of the gospel of Christ. Remember that in the last day, men will be judged according to his works. 1Peter 1:17, " And if ye call on the Father, who without respect of persons judgeth according to everyman's work, pass the time of your sojourning here in fear.

CHAPTER 9

The Laws Of Christ

The Law on Orderly Worship, Gifts of Tongues, and Prophecies

There are many worshippers in this Christian era who worship with the accompaniment of speaking in tongues and litany. This manner of worship is becoming utterly disorder and creating mere noise in the church. Some still practice speaking in tongues and prophesying in the midst church service. Everyone does not understand each other while others are shouting and uttering words nobody understands. There is neither an interpretation in what they utter as they believe and feel it is glorifying their way of worship.

And in some occasions from certain churches, church ministers and members tame the snakes believing that it would not bite them. Consequently, some who had attempted to hold it were killed and even the pastor who demonstrated in the presence of the church-members that he would not be bitten suffered the same fate as they were surprised that their belief did not work. Church cultures have become chaotic, confusing and destructive leaving no assurance of salvation for the innocent and pathetic followers.

Prophesying is misunderstood by those worshippers in a sense that they define or interpret this term only as " prediction of the events to come". *Prophesying* in the bible means *teaching the word of God.* To Prophesy is to teach . For information and confirmation , all prophecies can be found in the bible and have been prophesied by chosen people of God during the Old Testament until the coming of the Lord Jesus Christ.

They were the early prophets of God and disciples of Christ. Whatever predictions are being told now by bible teachers and preachers can be read in the bible. Phenomenal events and mysterious occurrences can be found in the bible such as the coming of Christ, the emergence of false prophets, murders and killings, persecution, long-sufferings, the phenomenal occurrences of earthquakes, sudden storms and typhoons, whirlwinds, tornados, volcanic eruptions, lunar and solar eclipses, war and rumors of wars in many countries and others.

Prophecies and predictions were written and foretold by the early prophets in the Old testament such as Isaiah, Samuel, Ezekiel, Daniel and others to mention. Other than that will have to scrutinize if it belongs to the bible. Certain verses in the bible will give us the definition of prediction which is foretelling and prophesying. In I Corinthians 14:5 says, " *I would that ye all spake with tongues, but rather that ye prophesied than he that speaketh with tongues, except he interpret, that the church may receive edifying.*" I Corinthians 14:3, " *But he that prophesieth speaketh unto men to edification, and exhortation and comfort.*"

In the said verses, speaking in tongues was encouraged if it can be interpreted by an interpreter of the one speaking in tongues and be understood by other believers, however, if nobody does it , it should not be done instead prophesy or teach the law of God in order to exhort and edify the church (worshippers). Speaking in tongues is not encouraged but rather prophesy as said in I Corinthians 14:6, " *Now, brothers, if I come to you and speak in tongues, what good will I be to you, unless I bring you some revelation or knowledge or prophesy or word of instructions or teachings.*"

Others may interpret prophesying as predicting or foretelling what is to come like a visionary or fortune teller. Nowadays, Fortune teller nor visionary does not play vital role in the bible but they appeared to be villains because their astrological activity is forbidden in the bible and is of the devil. Their predictions had been foretold in the bible as inspired by the devil. In fact, even today fortune telling is prohibited because they do not have certainties nor their predictions come into reality.

The bible has teachings concerning the orderly worship in the church. The bible also teaches that in the assembly of brethren, everyone should bring a hymn, an instruction, and a revelation. I Corinthians 14:26, " *how is it then brethren? When ye come together everyone of you hath a psalm, hath a doctrine, hath a tongue, hath a revelation, hath interpretation, let all things be done unto edifying.*" There is precisely a teaching about speaking in tongues.

The Law of Christ on Tithing

Is tithing of ten percent a law for the Christians nowadays ? Will a man rob God if he does not pay ten percent of his income? What is meant by tithes? Tithes is a form of payment which was commanded by God to the sons of Israel to bring into the house of the Levites in order to be used by the priesthood of the sons of Levi in the Old testament time. It was usually ten percent of the herd or livestock that could be consumed or used.

In Leviticus 27:30 reads, " *And all the tithe of the land, whether of the seed of the land, or of the fruit of the tree, is the Lord's; it is holy unto the Lord. And if a man will at all redeem aught of his tithes, he shall add thereto to the fifth part thereof. And concerning the tithe of the herd, or of the flock, even of whatsoever passeth under the rod, the tenth shall be holy unto the Lord, continue in Leviticus 27:34," These are the commandments, which the Lord commanded Moses for the children of Israel in mount Sinai.*" In other words, tithing was the command of God to Israel during that time.

Many Christian and even non-Christian churches today preach the tithing of ten percent in aid for the church. They teach the law of tithing ten percent as a valid law nowadays because the book of Malachi says so in chapter 3:10, " *Bring ye all the tithes into the storehouse, that there may be meat in mine house, and prove me now herewith, saith the Lord of hosts, if I will not open you the windows of heaven, and pour you out a blessing, that there shall not be room enough to receive it.*" The verse commanded to bring all the tithes into the storehouse then, if you don't, in Malachi 3:8-9, "Will a man rob God? Yet ye have robbed thee? In tithes and offerings. Ye are cursed with a curse: for ye have robbed me, even this whole nation."

The verse in Malachi 4:4 says, " *remember the law of my servant Moses, the decrees and laws, I gave him at Horeb for all Israel.*" This verse may be understood and confused by today's Christian believers as the law to be remembered and applied the application of tithing ten percent as it may justify the compulsory delivery of ten percent tithe offerings to the church. To reveal the misapplication of those verses today, we should ask first, For whom did God command that law?

The verse says, " for all Israel" Do present day believers belong to the house of Israel? In which era or time do we belong? We are not Israelites by race, nor we do belong to the house of Israel rather we belong to the Christian era. We are ethnically, non-Israelites, but from the roots of the Gentiles. Gentiles means races outside the house of Israel. Gentiles, as the bible teaches us are the heirs together with Israel in the promise in Christ Jesus.

To prove this allegation we can read this in *Ephesians 3:6*, " *This mystery is that through the gospel the Gentiles are heirs together with Israel, members together of one body, and sharer together in the promise in Christ Jesus.*" What is our testimony that we don't belong nor are we under the law of Moses? In *Acts 13:39*, " *and by him all that believe are justified from all things from which ye could not be justified by the law of Moses.*"

You will notice from the verse, the line that says, " you could not be justified from the law of Moses." This obviously means that we are no longer under the authority of the law of Moses. Christians do not have to follow this law because this was the for Israel. Nevertheless, they may not accept this verse until we support it with another verse to strengthen this claim. Accordingly, one will sin and rob God if he fails to obey this command.

Their claim can be read in *Malachi 3:8-10*, " *Will a man rob God? Yet you rob me. But you ask, how do we rob you? In tithes and offerings. You are under a curse- the whole nation of you because you are robbing me. Bring the whole tithe into the storehouse, that there may be food in my house, test me in this , says the Lord Almighty, and see if I will not throw open the floodgate of heaven and pour out so much blessings that you will not have room enough for it.*"

You must remove the feeling of guilt in you if you don't obey this command because this is not for you to obey but for the early Israelites or Hebrews at the time of Moses, for the sons and priests of the Levites. Furthermore to prove that this is not for present day believers, let us read *Matthew 23:23* " *Woe to you, teachers of the law and Pharisees, you hypocrites ! You give a tenth of your spices-mint, dill and cumin, But you have neglected the more important matters of the law – justice, mercy and faithfulness.*"

Believers could misunderstood the verse upon reading this line, " You should have practiced the latter, without neglecting the former" What is this line trying to point out? Is it the tithing of ten percent? What was being pointed out in this term "former"? With whom Jesus Christ was talking in this verse ? It is not the tithing of ten percent that was being pointed out here. Rather it is no other than: justice, mercy, and faithfulness.

Our Lord Jesus Christ was talking to the Pharisees and Scribes, who had been practicing the tithing of ten percent during that time. While this gives us awareness about the practice of the Pharisees and Scribes, what else do we expect more from Christ when he accused them of neglecting the more important things? Apparently, by analyzing the weight of this verse that Christ uttered to the Pharisees and Scribes, there is the presence of the accusation. Why? Because they were not doing what was right. If we would ask again, with whom did this verse is told to do? Let us read *Hebrew 7:5-12* , " *Now the law requires the descendants of Levi who become priests to collect a tenth from the people – that is, their brothers – even though their brothers are descended from Abraham.*" Verse 12 goes this way, " *For when there is a change of the priesthood, there must also be a change of the law.*"

In these two verses, a clarity in the statement is noticeable that the law was requiring the descendants of Levi to collect a tenth from their brothers and not from the Christians. In fact, the law has been changed when we read Hebrew 7:12 " *When there is a change of the priesthood, there must also be a change of the law.*" Take note of the clarity of the verse. Nowadays, What is the law in giving since the old law was changed or already repealed when Jesus Christ came to earth? The answer can be read in I *Corinthians 9:7*, " *Each man should give what he has decided in his heart to give, not reluctantly or under compulsion, for God loves a cheerful giver.*" This is a very clear verse in our time that commands us to give, what we have decided in our heart.

The apostle Paul was emphasizing in this verse that giving must come from the heart. Man's willingness to give without hesitance is one way of offering love and service to God. During the time of Jesus Christ there were many people who were already giving what they had decided in their hearts. We cannot say that this was tithing of 10%percent because in a particular scenario Jesus Christ saw the givers were not counting their offerings with ten percent instead they were depositing their money into the temple treasury.

Let us read this testimony in Mark 12:41, " *Jesus sat down opposite the place where the offerings were put and watched the crowd putting their money into the temple treasury. Many rich people threw in large amounts.*" The last line " *That people threw in large amounts.*" It is implied that as they got the money from their safe, they threw it right away in the treasury. Apparently, there was no accounting for ten percent, shall we then say that they had accounted for it when they went there?

It may not because most people then who were converted to Christianity knew the law of Moses on ten percent that they had to bring in their goods, crops and flocks and accounted for ten percent together with silver and coins. We should for a fact that the Pharisees are different from Christians when it comes to giving or offerings. They had laws to obey. Pharisees still had tithing of ten percent while

Christians have none, but they give according to the dictate of their hearts.

Although our Lord Jesus Christ had commanded those who taught and preached the gospel of salvation that they should live by the gospel, but not to the extent of abusing, enriching and living lavishly from the tithes of the church. Let us read the command in I Corinthians 9:7, " *Even so hath the Lord ordained that they which preach the gospel should live of the gospel*"

The apostle Paul despite the command to receive their living from the gospel did not make his living out of the church's tithes. He did not intend to be a burden to the church .Paul had to earn a living by selling tents while he preached the gospel. He struggled for the gospel and exerted efforts for a living. He experienced a great deal of sacrifice. His testimony can be read in I Corinthians 4:11 " *Even unto this present hour we both hunger and thirst, and are naked and are buffeted and have no certain dwelling place.*"

This verse testifies the reality of Christian sacrifice for the sake of Christ during those days. They were even persecuted, maltreated and separated from the world. Today, this really happens as it was said in the bible that in this world you will suffer tribulation and tribulation will become even more intensified in the last days and in the great tribulation

The Law of God on Believer's Manners and Conduct

The bible is not a mere book but a book which contains many laws of God to adhere with so that believers will be led to righteousness and to the path of salvation. The early Christians were taught to dress up properly when going to worship houses or center and even to this present day that law in fashion shall be obeyed by His followers. Modern day church-goers may not observe proper church dress code. It appears that in many churches today or the professed Christians do not observe proper wearing of attire. Let us read I *Timothy 2:9*, " *In like manner also, that women adorn themselves in modest apparel, with shamefulness and sobriety, not with braideth hair, or gold or pearls or costly array.*"

In fact you will notice that some women are indecently dressed up with an eye-catching attire enough to entice the lustful eyes of men. Apparently, women intentionally wear enticing attire with glitters in their parts of the body. It is not only indecent attire that the bible forbids but it warns us that women shall not wear the garments of men. However, nowadays, pants and shirts have been worn by both sexes and even women have their hair cut short while men have their hair long .

The book of *Deuteronomy 22:5*, says," *The women shall not wear that which pertaineth unto a man, neither shall a man put on a woman's garment; for all that do so are abomination unto the Lord thy God.*"

Nowadays, it is obviously not obeyed, instead men and women share the same kind of sin. Notice that hair of men now is grown long like that of women while women have their hair cut short like that of men. *1 Corinthians 11:14-15* say, " *Doth not even nature itself teach you, that, if a man have long hair, it is a shame unto him? But if a woman have long hair, it is a glory to her; for her hair is given her for a covering.*"

In these verses it is clearly said that long hair is only given to a woman for her covering while it is a shame for a man to have long hair. In some instances, indecent and seductive manner of wearing of garments by women cause men to sin. Naturally, from the lust of the eyes springs the lust of the flesh. *II Peter 2:14*, says," *having eyes full of adultery and that cannot cease from sin, beguiling unstable souls, a heart they have exercised with covetous practices, cursed children.*" Because of continues transgressions God gave them up to wicked kind of love.

The book of *Romans 1:26-27*, say, "*For this cause God gave them up unto vile affection; for even their women did change the natural use into that which is against nature; and likewise also the men, leaving the natural use of the women, burned in their lust one toward another men with men working that which is unseemly and receiving in themselves that recompense of them error which was meet.*"

While men and women turned away from their affection, men turn to men for affection and women to women. In the same manner that men have changed into a feminine behavior or the so-called swards, likewise the women, lesbians. The laws of Christ forbid women to wear tantalizing jewelries and precious gems while leading a Christian life. In the past, women of Zion are compared to women today because of their vanity, pride and arrogance in their attitudes and they were even assailed on their wearing much ornaments in their body.

Isaiah 3:16, 20,25 say, " Moreover the Lord saith, because the daughters of Zion are haughty and walk with stretched forth necks and wanton eyes, walking and mincing as they go, and making a tinkling with their feet; the bonnets and the ornaments of the legs, and the headbands, and the tablets, and the earrings. The rings, and nose jewels, the changeable suits of apparel, and the mantles, and the wimples, and the crisping pins. The glasses and the fine linen, and the hoods, and the veils. Thy men shall fall by the sword, and they mighty in the war." In the said verses, you will notice how women of Zion were described in their manners while these resulted to downfall of men.

The Law of Christ on Socializing with Unbelievers

Are you living with unbelievers? Do you mingle with unbelieving friends, relatives and family? Your husband nor your wife may not be a believer by this time but if you are a believer you may find a difficult time dealing with them and suffering a terrible situation. Your dilemma may not be ordinary with other Christian believers. The choice is, you get vexed and quit or you live and practice Christian virtues.

It may be said that it is easy to be a Christian but it is difficult to apply or live a Christian-like living. If you have an unbelieving wife or husband be extra careful in handling your situation or your marital affairs because religious indifferences can be a possible cause of separation. You may be annoyed because of your indifferences in principles but the bible instructs believers not to quit nor leave a husband or wife.

Let us read, I Corinthians 13:14," *And the woman which hath a husband that believeth not, and if he be pleased to dwell with her, let her not leave him. For the unbelieving husband is sanctified by the wife, and the unbelieving wife is sanctified by the husband; else were your children unclean; but now are they holy.*"

More Laws in the Christian Era

If you believe in the Ten Commandments of God given to Moses and His people where certain commandments such as the observance of Sabbath is no longer followed by many Christian groups today. We should realize that the Old Testament laws have been changed in the New Testament during the time of Jesus Christ. According to *Hebrew 8:13*," *In that he saith, A new covenant, he hath made the first old. Now that which decayeth and waxeth old is ready to vanish away.*" The verse is very clear that a new covenant (teachings or laws) has made the old one vanished away.

During the time of Jesus Christ the Ten Commandments which the Jews believed and Christians follow and know in this present dispensation have become more than ten because of Christ's laws taught to his followers then and now. In the old Ten Commandments, one of the commandments is, respect your father and mother; but Christ taught to all Christians, respect all men. It means that is not only your Father and Mother you are bound to pay respect but all men.

They may be your brothers, sisters, elderly and all men. *(1Peter 2:17, "Honor all men. Love the brotherhood. Fear God, Honor the king.")* Sometimes persons bound themselves to respect only their parents but not others, that is why during the Christian era it was commanded to respect all men. Realistically, that is one added commandment that Christ has taught us.

Another commandments added are: In the Old testament, one commandment is: Do not kill; in the New testament killing a person has become stricter because when you *harbor hatred* in your heart against anybody it is tantamount to killing him. In the Ten Commandments the command is: Do not kill. In the New Testament, the commandment is; *do not hate nor harbor hatred against anybody.*

In the Old Testament, the early Jews observed the Sabbath. They did not work during Sabbath day nor strictly did anything that might break its observance. But in the Christian dispensation, Sabbath is no longer observed but rather the Christians are instructed to gather to worship in the first day of the week which is Sunday in our present calendar. Even Jesus did good in Sabbath day when he helped and healed the sick. Did He not render his services on that very Sabbath day? He did and broke the Sabbath. Therefore, it is not absolute that you strictly observe it when it will ask you to render something worthy for others and for God. The bible says in *Acts 20:7, And upon the first day of the week, when the disciples came together to break bread, Paul preached unto them, ready to depart on the morrow, and continued his speech until midnight;*" Christ also defied the Sabbath by doing good or performing Samaritan work. In *John 5:18 says, " Therefore the Jews sought the more to kill him, because he not only had broken the Sabbath, but said also that God was his Father, making himself equal with God.*" Another added laws today is the eating of those four-legged animals and cloven-footed. Leviticus 11:2-7, read, " Speak unto the children of Israel, saying, These are the beasts that are on the earth. Whatsoever parteth the hoof, and is cloven-footed, and cheweth the cud, among the beasts, that shall ye eat. Nevertheless, these shall ye not eat of them that chew the cud, or of them that divide the hoof: as the camel, because he cheweth the cud, but divideth not the hoof; he is unclean unto you.

And the coney, because he cheweth the cud, but divideth not the hoof; he is unclean unto you. And the hare, because he cheweth the cud, but divideth not the hoof; he is unclean unto you. And the swine, though he divide the hoof, and be cloven-footed, yet he cheweth not the cud; he is unclean to you."

The early Israelites were forbidden to eat the said beasts that were cloven-footed such as the pigs, carabaos, rabbits, cows and other cloven-footed animals. But in the present dispensation, they are already allowed by Christ's law to be consumed because they are already cleansed. Mark 7:19, "because it entereth not his heart, but into the belly, and goeth out , into the draught, purging all meats." Therefore, what is crucial in this verse is the thing that enters our hearts, and not the meats that we eat.

Even the Apostle Peter was urged to eat these cloven-footed beasts when he got hungry. In Acts. 10:10-16 " and he became very hungry, and would have eaten; but while they made ready, he fell into a trance, and saw heaven opened, and a certain vessel descending unto him, as it had been a great sheet knit at the four corners, and let down to the earth: wherein were all manner of four-footed beasts of the earth, and wild beasts, and creeping things, and fowls of the air. And there came a voice to him, Rise, Peter; kill, and eat. But Peter said, Not so, Lord; for I have never eaten anything that is common or unclean. And the voice spake unto him again the second time, What God hath cleansed, that call not thou common. This was done thrice; and the vessel was received up again into heaven."

Another added commandment of Christ is the giving of tithes; in the book of *Malachi 3: 6-11. And in Hebrew 7:5-12* , " *Now the law requires the descendants of Levi who become priests to collect a tenth from the people – that is, their brothers – even though their brothers are descended from Abraham.*" Verse 12 goes this way, " For when there is a change of the priesthood, there must also be a change of the law."

In other words, the old law which was the law for the Hebrews or Israelites particularly of the Leviticus priesthood had been changed today. The Christian law that should be followed by believers is that you give what your heart decides. This is the command in 2*Corinthians 9:7*, " *Each man should give what he has decided in his heart to give, not reluctantly or under compulsion, for God loves a cheerful giver.*" This is a very clear verse in our time that commands us to give, what we have decided in our heart. Another Christian law today that we should know is when a man stares with lust and sexual desire to a woman that man has impliedly sins already of adultery.

There are other Christian laws and teachings that we may say more than the laws of the Ten Commandments received by Moses in Mt. Sinai. One very significant law of Christ today which is not in the Ten Commandments is the Baptism in water which is the commandment for all Christians that we are obliged to fulfill. According to *Galatians 6:2, " Bear ye one another's burden, and so fulfill the law of Christ"* Other laws which are prohibited by the law of Christ are :

The imposition of usurious interest in lending and illegal works such as gambling, selling illegal drugs, pornography, smuggling, graft and corruption and many more acts constituting crime. Who prepare the food for the idols? The Gentiles who do not know God prepare the foods for the idols and it shall not be eaten by believers(occasions such as fiestas , moon festivals and other festivities concerning idols, patrons and sorts of worship in graven images) as the bible warns in 1Corinthians 10:20, it reads " *But I say, that the things which the Gentiles sacrifice, they sacrifice to devils, and not to God, and I would not that ye should have fellowship with the devils*"

It is clearly stated verbatim and conclusively one of the sins against the Holy Ghost. What are these idols in which the forbidden foods are offered? They are idols in which men worship, pray and kneel down before. Even in the past men sinned because they worshipped graven images. In *Proverbs 115: 4-7* read, " *Their idols are silver and gold, the work of men's hands. They have mouths, but they speak not: eyes have they, but they see not; they have ears; but they hear not: noses have they, but they smell not; they have hands; but they handle not; fee have they, but they walk not; neither speak they through their throat." What are the foods that believers should eat without sinning*?

In the past, God mentioned those foods that should be eaten by His people and those foods that they should not eat. The commandment is clear on eating meat but there is an exception as stated in *Genesis 9:3-4.* " *Every moving things that liveth shall be meat for you; even as the green herb have I given you all things, But flesh with life thereof, which is the blood thereof, shall ye not eat.*" Notice that blood is forbidden by God to be eaten by His people as this commandment is still subsisting today.

The Believing and Non-Believing Couples

If a wife has an unbelieving husband, the bible teaches the wife not to separate nor leave her husband. In 1Corinthians 7:10-11, say, " *And unto the married I command yet not, but the Lord, Let not the wife depart from her husband: but and if she depart, let her remain unmarried, or be reconciled to her husband; and let not the husband put away his wife.*" The verse clearly tells that if a wife departs her husband she should not marry but reconcile in due time with the latter and the husband should not depart his wife as well.

I Corinthians 7:12-14 says, " *But to the rest speak, I, not the Lord: If any brother hath a wife that believeth not, and she be pleased to dwell with him, let him not put her away. And the woman which hath a husband that believeth not, and if he be pleased to dwell with her, let her not leave him. For the unbelieving husband is sanctified by the wife, and the unbelieving wife is sanctified by the wife, else were your children unclean; but now are they holy.*"

Therefore, the one who leaves the other should not initiate marrying other man or woman, but she/he remains unmarried but the one who is left alone has the right to re-marry. This law is applied also under civil law on family relations of Civil Code. In the observance of Christian living, a husband and wife should give each other a chance to avail each other personal and religious freedom. Religious freedom should not be impaired according to the Constitution, while criminal law punishes the offender who compels his husband or wife to embrace his or her religion. However, this provision of law has always been abused without any complaint by the offended person.

This may be done in such a way that compulsion to adhere with one's belief is not made a reason for separation but in some other reason husband and wife part their ways. In employment, this is also abused but not apparently made as the ground for a person's expulsion particularly in local companies where the culture emphasizes adherence to their religious practices or beliefs, otherwise, an applicant or employee can be terminated constructively.

But the essence of conjugal partnership according to the teaching of God is that relationship between husband and wife should have righteousness, judgment and in loving-kindness, and in mercies, and faithfulness. Both of them should know righteousness which is the Word of God, correct judgment where both always apply sound and righteousness in time of controversy as to family affairs, one should not favor unfairly but instead weigh and qualify each party's contention; love and kinds should always take place with harmony and understanding among the family members with mercies at all times and the wife and husband should observe faithfulness that serves as the foundation of maintaining a stable family institution.

The bible attests to this fact in *Hosea 2:19-20, "And I will betroth thee unto me in righteousness, and in judgment, and in loving-kindness, and in mercies. I will even betroth thee unto me in faithfulness; and thou shalt know the LORD"*

There are some church's culture where members do not associate or socialize intimately with those non church-members because of differences in culture and beliefs. Consequently, there are those who treat others unkindly, superficially and maliciously. Are Christian-believers forbidden by Christ to live, associate or socialize with non-Christians? How do Christians interact in society full of multi-cultural & religious beliefs ? Of course, mixed society is full of strangers with exotic beliefs

Even the apostle Paul, a disciple of Christ associated with the Gentiles in propagating the gospel associated with non-believers. Let us read 1 Corinthians 9: 19-22, "*For though be free from all men, yet have I made myself servant unto all, that I might gain the more. And I unto the Jews I became as a Jew, That I might gain the Jews; to them that are under the law, as under the law, that I might gain them that are without law, as without law, (being not without law to God, but under the law to Christ) that I might gain them that are without law. To the weak became I as weak, that I might gain the weak: I am made all things to all men, that I might by all means have some.*"

Therefore, the apostle Paul associated with the unbelievers for the sake of the gospel. But the mere intention of Apostle Paul was to win them in the Lord. There must be a purpose why Christians associate most of the time today with non-believers. It may be for different motives, such as mere gatherings and acquaintances, friendship, business, spiritual and many other reasons they themselves believe.

Being a friend to the Gentiles is not a problem because believers are tasked also to show them the kind of faith they have in Christ . And for that purpose believers may lead them to the same faith. However, in socializing with the unbelievers the bible warns not to conform to their unwanted ways because Christians received the law of Christ not to touch or dwell unclean things from them. This is proven in Colossians 4:5 that reads, " *Walk in wisdom toward them that are without, reckoning the time.*" There is a better way that believers could get along with the unbelievers and that is mingling with them with wisdom.

Believers with wisdom in socializing with unbelievers know what to do even they are surrounded with temptations that may drag them to sin. The apostle Paul said in I Timothy 3:15, "*but if I tarry long, that those mayest know how those oughtest to behave thyself in the house of God, which is the church of the living God, the pillar and ground of the truth.*"God knows who His people are even in the midst of many believers, those who are faithful and those who turned away from their faith.

Faithful believers always keep on praying with thanksgiving. This is attested in I Timothy 2:1-2, "*I exhort therefore, that, first of all, supplications, prayers, intercourse and giving of thanks, be made for all men; kings, and for all that are in authority, that we may lead a quiet and peaceful life in all godliness and honesty.*" God's people avoid all forms of inequities and evil thoughts in the midst of persecution and temptations.

In 2Timothy 2:19 reads, "*Nevertheless the foundation of God standeth sure, having this seal, the Lord knoweth them that are his: And, let everyone that nameth the name of Christ depart from iniquity.*"

Importance of Baptism

What is baptism? Who should be baptized? What is the proper way of baptizing and how is it done? Baptism is immersion into the water which signifies the cleansing of the one being baptized from spiritual filthiness, thereby, renewing the spirit to a new one. When a person is baptized he is given a new spirit which is called the inner man. Accordingly, a person is baptized in the name of Jesus Christ, and receiving the gifts of the Holy Spirit .

The inner man is a new spirit that worships God. Baptism is done where there is plenty of flowing waters that will wash away the filthy spirits that may come out of the one being baptized when he or she is immersed. By Baptism, our sins are cleansed. Let us read *Acts 22:16*, "*And now why tarriest thou? Arise, and be baptized, and wash away thy sins, calling on the name of the Lord.*" When you have been baptized you are converted into Christian and you should be called Christian.

Let us read *Acts 11:26*, " *and when he had found him, he brought him unto Antioch. And it came to pass, that a whole year they assembled themselves with the church, and taught much people. And the disciples were called Christians first in Antioch.*" Immersion into the water is very important for the spirit cleansing of an individual and it should not just be done by sprinkling of water in the head of the ones being baptized. Baptism is only applicable to adult ones who believe in the teachings of Christ and not to infants because the ones who are to be baptized have to be cleansed from his sins while the infants have not sinned so they should not be baptized.

As we all know, infants are innocent and sin-free human beings. They are of God and even if they die in their infancy they will go to heaven. The kingdom of heaven belongs to them. One cannot be a Christian without being baptized because it is through baptism by which a Christian-convert is cleansed of his sins and can receive Jesus Christ and the gift of the Holy Spirit according to the bible.

Let us read *Acts 2:38,* " Then Peter said unto them, Repent, and be baptized every one of you in the name *of Jesus Christ for the remission of sins, and ye shall receive the gift of the Holy Ghost.*" This verse tells the forgiveness of sins from the beginning they are committed until the time they are asked for forgiveness. When a sinful man repents penitently and opens his heart to receive baptism in the name of Jesus Christ, the gift from the Holy Spirit shall also be received as we begin to live a new life. Through baptism the promise in the word of God that the one baptized shall have a new life is fulfilled.

In Romans 6:4 says. " *Therefore we are buried with him by baptism into death; that like as Christ was raised up from the dead by the glory of the Father, even so we also should walk in newness of life.*" The old self is buried upon immersion into the water as we resurrect for a new life, therefore, a newly-baptized individual shall now be called Christian. He now lives as a new creature and all things in the past must be forgotten and abandoned. New things for a Christian are new. After baptism, an individual becomes a Christian. This is attested in II Corinthians "*Therefore if any man be in Christ, he is a new creature; old things are passed away: behold, all things are become new.*"

In the book of Matthew, we will notice that Jesus Christ went to Jordan river and asked John to be baptized. Why did he have to be baptized when in fact He did not commit any sin? Definitely, He did not sin and was no sinner. He asked John to baptize him in order to receive the Spirit of God while it was also a situation that the Father introduced him as His Son.

Significantly, it shows that baptism is defined for those who would be baptized that they would receive Jesus Christ and the gift from Holy Ghost that the Father from heaven is sending. Let us read to prove the statement in Matthew 3:13-16. " The cometh Jesus from Galilee to Jordan unto John to be baptized of him. But John forbade him, saying, I have need to be baptized of thee, and comest thou to me? And, Jesus answering said unto him,

Suffer it to be so now; for this it becometh us to fulfill all righteousness, then he suffered him. And Jesus, when he was baptized, went ;up straight way out of the water, and lo, the heavens were opened unto him, and he saw the Spirit of God descending like a dove, and lighting upon him, and a voice from heaven, saying, " This is my beloved Son, in whom I am well pleased."

CHAPTER 10

The Teachings on Life after Death

Is there life after death? What happens to man's soul and spirit after death?

Some religious people believe and say that soul of a dead man goes to heaven once he dies if he is good and in hell if he is bad. Others believe in the saying that a dead man goes back to his house and his family after three days. It becomes the typical and customary beliefs of people who have not read nor heard the teachings of Christ about life after death. It is a baseless and false belief that is not founded by the Word. The succeeding lines are unfounded and man-made beliefs : Some éstablished practices of people are done by offering candles in the dead man's grave believing that it would serve them food for them. Others would even serve different kinds of fruits which after the event would be eaten when left by living men passing by. The truth is , some accustomed practices were observed without biblical foundation. Others do not mind whether if it is biblical or not. What is important to them is that they have served its purpose. But a Christian faith is far from this kind of practices because Christian- believers are taught the teachings of Christ. We must bear in mind that the bible teaches us this verse in *Luke 4:4*, " *Man does not live by bread alone*." Meaning we have to read and study the word of God which serves as our spiritual food, but not the material food we eat for our physical nourishment and living. Referring to Ecclesiastes 12:7, the said verse explicitly tells what happens to humans when they die.

We should know the teachings of God in the bible. We live by the word as we live by the food we eat. The Word is the food of our soul and spirit. If we don't know anything about the word in the bible your soul will dry up and you may be lead spiritually empty. You have to feed your soul and spirit with the Word of God in order to worship Him who gives life. Let us read Hebrew 9:27, "*And as it is approved unto men once to die, but after this the judgment.*"

There is only one day for a man to be judged whether he deserves to be in heaven or in hell in the judgment day. The verse quoted is not an immediate judgment when a person dies. The verse tells that men are destined for one day judgment after dying. It means all nations will be gathered together before the judgment seat of God. *Matthew 25:32-33* say, " *and before him shall be gathered all nations: and he shall separate them one from another, as a shepherd divideth his sheep from the goats: and he shall set the sheep on his right hand, but the goats on the left.*"

Another verse that will support my allegation of the one day judgment can be read in *Acts 17:31* which says, " *because he hath appointed a day, in the which he will judge the world in righteousness by that man whom he hath ordained; whereof he hath given assurance unto all men, in that he hath raised him from the dead.*" Take note in the verse "appointed a day" which means that there is one day for all to be judged. What is the proof that we will all have to wait for one judgment day ? Let us read *Acts 17:31*, " *God has set a day when he will judge the world with justice by the man He has appointed (Jesus Christ).*" This is clear now that a certain day is set for mankind to be judged by our God.

Is there really a Paradise? Where is it? Yes, there is. It can be found in the third (3rd) heaven. *2 Corinthians 12:2-4," I knew a man in Christ above fourteen years ago,(whether in the body, I cannot tell; or whether out of the body, I cannot tell. God knoweth) such a one caught up to the third heaven."* Paradise was promised by Christ to a dying criminal on the cross. *Luke 23:42-43 says," And he said unto Jesus, Lord," remember me when thou comest into thy kingdom. And Jesus said unto him, Verily I say unto thee, Today, shalt thou be with me in paradise."*

And this same paradise was a promise to all who will be saved. *Titus 1:2,says* " In hope of eternal life, which God, that cannot lie, promised before the world began." It is also in Paradise also where we can see the water of life and the tree of life. That is in *Revelation 22:1-3, "And he showed me a pure river of water of life, clear as crystal, proceeding out of the throne of God and of the Lamb. In the midst of the street of it, and on either side of the river, was there the tree of life, which bare twelve manner of fruits, and yielded her fruit every month; and the leaves of the tree were for the healing of the nations."*

When one will be saved in the last day he will be given a white stone where it contains his new name. In Revelation 2:17," He that hath an ear, let him hear what the Spirit saith unto the churches? To him that overcometh will I give to eat of the hidden manna and will give him a white stone and in the stone a new name written which no man knoweth saving he that receiveth." Hence, the overcomer or the triumphant will be with the Lord. Revelation 3:4," Thou hast a few names even in Sardis which have not defiled their garments; and they shall walk with in white; for they are worthy."

Cause of Spiritual Death

Many people have been misled by false teachings because of lack of knowledge and they have not tested the spirits of the doctrines of the preacher. Hosea 4:6 says," *My people are destroyed from lack of knowledge*."It is quoted in the bible that when the blind leads another blind, both of them will fall into a pit. The term "blind" refers to an innocent and unknowledgeable person.

This statement is supported by this verse in Matthew 15:14, " *Leave them; they are blind guides. If a blind man leads a blind man, both will fall into a pit.*" If the bible warns us of the emergence of false prophets in the last days it also encourages and strengthens us with promising word of God. Days are evil, says the bible and we ought to strengthen our faith by knowing the Word that will shield and teach us what to do in these dangerous times. Certain verses in the bible will give knowledge about exhortations to Christians. Ephesians 6:10-11, read " *Finally; be strong in the Lord and His mighty power, Put on the full armor of God so that you can take your stand against the devil's schemes.*"

Perhaps, many church-goers who are used to rituals and sermons of their church leader do not know that the key to spiritual strength is knowing the Word when taught correctly. By hearing the correct teachings, faith in the word makes one to be alive. Christians grow and become mature spiritually and eventually changing their minds into righteousness. There are many teachers of faith who claim they are sent to preach the gospel and show wonders and miracles to people proving they are sent by God.

If one will take a look at the bible, in Matthew 13:22, " *For false Christ and false prophets will appear and perform signs and miracles to deceive even the elect, if that were possible.*" This verse tells clearly that those who perform these wonders and miracles are deceivers. People must see to it that they are not deceived by these signs, otherwise, your faith will be in danger. A man of faith has an infallible knowledge about the word if he claims to be a teacher of faith. If false teachers are claiming that their teachings come from God what more to an appointed teacher who has an infallible word and truth. People must know that the chosen one should have the fruits of the Holy Spirit and these are manifested in his way of living.

False teachers will even convince people of their miracles and wonders. People will be amazed if they see miracles and wonders happen. We remember that false prophets are instruments of the devil to show wonders and miracles. In Matthew 24:24, " *For Christ and false prophets will appear and perform great signs and miracles to deceive even the elect – if that is possible.*" It does not follow that wonders and miracles nowadays are credible. Other teachers of religion could even discourage members of the church from consulting physicians when sick and if necessary they will avoid taking modern medicines to be cured and healed.

They would cast out diseases and other forms of illnesses from the body of a person instead. The miracles that God does, nowadays are not in the forms of those amazing spectacles and phenomena. Our daily survival in life's struggle as we see ourselves alive again the next day, is one miracle that most people don't realize. The strength and peaceful living that we enjoy daily is another miracle. When we go out of the house and go somewhere else and get back alive is another miracle. A person may not know what will happen when he goes out there along the road or wherever he may be that all of sudden a lunatic or a rascal may injure or kill him.

Or when you go out in the busy street you might get side-swiped by a running vehicle, but when you run to and fro unscathed even to the remote places on earth and get back alive and well is already a miracle. Is that not a miracle when we all survive getting along in the world of strangers every day? Who say that we do not believe in God's miracles ?

It is not that we don't believe in God's miracles. The things is, God is doing miracles to all of us every day but people just don't notice and acknowledge them. It is God who heals and cures diseases. It is God who provides our daily living and survival. God is instrumental in doing miracles in people's lives. But the sad thing is, false teachers make miracles for themselves to amaze people. They are doing strange spectacles that will convince people to believe him. We should know that modern science and technology help a lot in the progress and advancement of our civilization.

There are religious and fanatic people who would criticize and interpret the development in modern technology as the work of the devil. An example of their misinterpretation is the development and use of card system in buying and withdrawing money in banks as sign that the anti-Christ inspire its emergence.

How come when it is practically being used for people's convenience? We should understand that civilization is heading to its progress and it advances as population grow tremendously every year. People have to think of ways to improve ways of living. We should realize that these things would not happen if it were not God's will like the discovery of medicines for cure in certain incurable diseases. In the book of Ecclesiastes 3:10-11, say " *I have seen the thing beautiful in its time.* He has also set eternity in the hearts of men; yet they cannot fathom what God has done from beginning of end."

In King James version it says, " I have seen the travail, which God hath given to the sons of men to be exercised in it. He hath made everything beautiful in his time; also he hath set the world in their heart, so that no man can find out the work that God maketh from the beginning to the end." However, in the Pilipino rendition of this verse what was given to men was diseases and illnesses in which men should find the proper cure and remedy. In other words, problems like this one is allowed by God to exist in order for men to study and explore for survival. Notice the growth and advancement in science and technology that men are trying to explore and discover. Are they not of necessities for men ?

On the other hand, *James 5:14-15* teach us this way," *Is any one of you sick? He should call the elders of the church to pray over him and anoint him with oil in the name of the Lord. And the prayer offered in faith will make a sick person well; the Lord will raise him up.*" In the said verses, anointing of oil in the Name of the Lord to a sick person refers here to teachings of Christ and not the oil per se (not the literal oil) but the Word of God being taught in the bible as the elders pray for him. Faith in Christ is indoctrinated in the bible by the first Apostles of Jesus Christ.

The first disciples who received the doctrine of faith in Christ gave their lives for the sake of Christ. Other religious groups and even cults have also indoctrination of faith from their leaders. Some of them would even kill because of the faith they receive. Faith comes from the kind of doctrines the leaders teach their followers.

While false teachings are rampant more false teachers appear. The emergence of these deceivers will be accompanied and supported by amazing wonders and miracles. Another instance in which people are misled in the interpretation of the verse in the bible is the people's understanding in *John 10:10*, "*The thief comes only to steal and kill and destroy; I have come that they may have life,; and have it to the full.*"

They believe that the thief being referred here is Satan because Satan, in their understanding; steals, kills and destroys. In the final analysis, the thief being pointed out here is the ordinary man who steals, kills and destroys. How did we know that it is an ordinary man? Let us read John 10:1, "*I tell you the truth, the man who does not enter the sheep pen by the gate, but climbs in by some other way, is a thief and a robber.*" Is it not the thief who is a man who does not enter by the gate but by some other way? His intention is to steal, kill if cornered by the police or the owners of the house shall destroy all possible means to get his way out to escape or fight back to be able to ran away.

On the other hand, certain religious groups assert that Satan causes men to get sick and killed. We would like to rectify these wrong notion, as we asserts that a certain verse in the bible attests to the fact that ironically, God is the One who is doing all these things to men. In Deuteronomy 32: 39, reads " *See now that I, even I, am he, and there is no god with me; I kill, and I make alive; I wound, and I heal; neither is there any that can deliver out of my hand.*" The verse affirms that God is the One who takes the life of a man and causes him to get sick.

If we believe that God is powerful than Satan, then God allows and does not allow certain things to happen. Therefore, God has the sole power to cause all things to happen and not to happen. The proof can be read in the book of Job. When Job was put into test, God warned Satan not to touch Job, but only allowed certain things to happen like the infliction of wounds in Job's body. People have reasons why they die and why they get sick. Observe those people who are physically weak but do not die and those who are strong but die soon. In other words, God has the sole will to allow us live and die and to make us ill and strong.

In many parts of the world, famine, natural calamities and wars are destroying human beings and their habitats. The bible warns mankind that this is just the beginning, but not yet the end. We shall experience tribulation on earth.

Satan & his Angels and the Worst of Men

The story of creation in the book of Genesis tells that heavens (there are three (3) heavens, *2 Corinthians 12:2*) and earth were created by God and everything that is in it. In the same way that God also created all the angels including Lucifer who was called the Morning Star. Stars in the bible represent the angels. They were also given free will by God to know what is right and wrong. Lucifer became ambitious that he wanted to be like God. He commanded his cohorts to rebel and consequently, he was thrown down from heaven with his cohorts by God .

Let us read the fact in Isaiah 14:12-14, " How art thou fallen from heaven, O Lucifer, son of the morning! How art thou cut down to the ground, which didst weaken the nations! For thou hast said in thine heart, I will ascend into heaven, I will exalt my throne above the stars of God: I will sit also upon the mount of the congregation, in the sides of the north: I will ascend above the heights of the clouds; I will ascend above the heights of the clouds; I will be like the Most High."

In the said verses, we will notice how Lucifer aspired to equal and be like God in his ambition which was cut or aborted that resulted to his downfall. When they were cast down to the ground, they sowed and continuously sow evil and wickedness among men. They even possessed men with unclean and evil spirits. They tempt men to do evil and detestable things on earth. In fact the serpent which symbolizes Satan tempted Adam & Eve in the garden of Eden who allowed sin to enter them, thus, the first sin was committed by them that caused them out of Eden.

Satan and his cohorts in the spirits have the power to transform in different forms that continuously tempt, scare and drive mankind to destruction. Satan is even said by the bible to be acting as an angel of light. *2 Corinthians 11:14 " And no marvel; for Satan himself is transformed into an angel of light. Therefore it is no great thing if his ministers also be transformed as the ministers also be transformed as the ministers of righteousness; whose end shall be according to their works."*

In other words, Satan and his cohorts in the spirits can enter into a human body particularly in the minds of the people, that is why, those people who have the so-called evil minds perform evil things. They let themselves to be used by the works of the devil. It is true, Idle mind is the devil's workshop. No wonder there are those evil doers who rob, steal, kill, murder, corrupt, do heinous crimes and other sorts of detestable works are rampant on earth, and even worse than before because of the evil spirits that drive them to do so.

We may even think that Satan and his cohorts are evil spirits which drive and tempt people to commit sins, therefore, we, human beings have the power also and capacity to resist those temptations that they offer ,thereby saving us from sins.

In other words, we cannot dwell in sins if we resist them and live a happy and sin-free life. Therefore, the main objective of Satan and cohorts is to drive or tempt human beings to sin and destruction. Since they are spirit beings they can dwell in our minds as they drive us to evil works. We human beings, therefore, have the free will to know and do what is right and wrong. So, if we choose wrong and walk to a wicked path, we perish. But if we choose right, we choose life, then we live. Man's free will has the power of control over those temptations. We may think therefore, that since we are the *doer* of the actions that are being dictated to us by Satan and his evil spirits we tend to become worst as the case may be. We may also think that since *man is* in the physical being who performs the perpetration of crime being dictated by Satan may even become worst than Satan because Satan is only a dictator and not a doer (because he is not in the flesh or physical being) is already judged to be in hell in the day of judgment.

Notice that there are unbearable heinous crimes that evil men do against men. There are heinous crimes that evil me do like slaughtering of human flesh which is unbearable and could hardly imagine and some may never think in their wildest dream that it can be done. Those evil men are already numb and animals, we can term it that way. Since we all know for a fact that Satan, the leader of all abominable works, together with his cohorts are trying to sow abominations and to gain allies among evil men on earth. But we, who are still alive and wanted by Satan to be his cohorts, have the power to resist them. That is why the bible instructs us to resist the devil so that they may flee from us and do not entertain evil works in your mind.

James 4:7, says " Submit yourselves therefore to God. Resist the devil, and he will flee from you." Take note that Satan is a great teaser or pusher of mankind to commit abominable acts. Men are the actors and performers in the perpetration of sins. Satan is a pusher and Man is the performer, who has been given the free will whether to choose the right and wrong thing while he has the capacity to resist the devil. Man will be liable for the consequences of his wrong choice in the end if he chooses wrong. Remember that Adam and Eve were given free will to choose which is right and which is wrong. They were told not to eat the fruit of the tree of sin as they allowed the serpent which tempted them to commit sin. They sinned because they allowed sin to enter their lives. Therefore, they chose sin and as a consequence they were ousted from the garden of Eden.

If you are a learned Christian you have realized that we should always be vigilant and aware that there are unseen evil spirits around us and they are always ready to devour us. 1 Peter 5:8, says, " Be sober, be vigilant; because your adversary the devil, as a roaring lion, walketh about, seeking whom he may devour"

Compositions of a Human Being

Many people believe that there is something in a man that separates him after death though world religions have developed a bewildering array of beliefs about the hereafter. Something inside a person is immortal and goes on living after departing. According to the Holman Illustrated Bible Dictionary, "soul is equated with the total person." In Genesis 2:7 states, " God proceeded to form the man out of dust from the ground and to blow into his nostrils the breath of life, and the man came to be a living soul. The first man , Adam was a soul." In other words, when man was created, he was composed of dust from the ground and the breath of life which is the spirit that God gave us. This spirit which makes us alive returns to God when a man dies.

The understanding that the word "soul" can mean the whole being of a person is supported by other scriptures. The bible speaks of a soul. In Leviticus 23:30, "The soul is spoken of as being impatient, irritated, sleepless, fearful, and depressed. Romans 13:1 states : " Let every soul be in subjection to the superior authorities." And at I Peter 3:20, we read: " In Noah's days, a few people, that is, eight souls were carried safely through the water." Apparently, it does not mention any soul that is some immaterial entity that lives on after death. The terms "soul" and "life" are used in parallel, one amplifying the meaning of the other. " Soul", then, can also refer to the life that one enjoys as a living soul, or person. The bible refers to Moses' enemies who were seeking to take his life as "all the men who were hunting for |his} soul." (Exodus 4:19) , Matthew 20:28 reads, " And concerning Jesus Christ, the bible says: " The Son of Man came to give his soul {life} a ransom in exchange for many."

While man has three compositions as affirmed in the bible such as spirit, soul and body. The bible tells in 1 Thessalonians 5:23, "And the very God of peace sanctify you wholly; and I pray God your whole spirit and soul and body be preserved blameless unto the coming of our Lord Jesus Christ.", we can say that man's composition will only become two because in Genesis 2:7, it is stated there that man is made up of dust and the breath of life which is the spirit that God gave us. And after that man became a living soul.

The soul is the wholeness or entirety of a human being that makes soul and body as one. When this soul has no spirit from God it is lifeless, meaning the spirit that is dead in Christ, the one that is of the world which is full of sin . But when a man is given a new spirit when baptized, he becomes a living soul with a new spirit. A man without a spirit of God is dead according to the bible and he is only pronounced alive when he is renewed or living a new life in Christ.

Therefore, having a new spirit a man lives and now contains three compositions; spirit and soul and body. Those who continuously live in sins in this world are not given a spirit but they merely live in their body and soul because they are dead in their faith and therefore, spiritless. The body that has no spirit is dead although living in the body and soul. They have no spirit from God because they have no faith. Faith without works is dead according to James 2:17,"Even so faith, if it hath not works, is dead, being alone." This spirit that the bible is referring when given unto man will help him in many things, example is his weaknesses.

Romans 8:26,says " Likewise the Spirit also helpeth our infirmities: "The reason they live is because of the breath of life which is different from the spirit of the sons of God. In Judas 1:19

read, " These be they who separate themselves, sensual, having not the Spirit." Men should have a clean heart and renewed spirit in order to have complete compositions. Psalms 51:10 says " Create in me a clean heart, O God; and renew a right spirit within me."

The Perfect Man

In the Old Testament time, Job was a perfect man. Perfect means blameless and upright. The bible accounts another perfect man in the bible, in Genesis 6: 9, " This is the account of Noah. Noah was a righteous man, blameless among the people of his time, and ;he walked with God." Do perfect men exist nowadays ? The bible will answer in James 3:2, " We all stumble in many ways. If anyone is never at fault in what he says, he is a perfect man, able to keep his whole body in check." If anyone is like the one mentioned in the said verse he must be a perfect man. The apostle Paul during his ministry took a long journey to bring the gospel of salvation. He sacrificed and almost died on his way to the mission. This was the way Paul served God because the gospel that he brought to the people was the gospel of Christ.

He strictly warned the other workers and those who heard the gospel of Christ that others would emerge with different teachings. This warning can be read in Galatians 1:8, " But even if we, or an angel from heaven should preach a gospel other than the one we preached to you, let him be eternally condemned." In this case, Paul commanded to search and test all the spirits if it is from God in order not to be misled in the hearing the word of God.. Don't just believe to what you hear. Prove it in the bible. 1John 4:1, says, " Beloved, believe not every spirit, but try the spirits whether they are of God, because many false prophets are gone out into the world." Every spirit refers to the teachings of the Preachers. Test it by affirming the verses in the bible if they are present and existing.

As it is said in Matthew 5:20, " For I tell you that unless your righteousness surpasses that if the Pharisees and teachers of the law you will certainly not enter the kingdom of heaven."Are there still Pharisees and Scribes nowadays ? There are many of them today. In fact, they preach in large crowd without knowing that their teachings do not conform with the teachings of Jesus Christ. Perhaps, some are aware that they have false teachings, but they hide it for themselves for certain reasons.

Angels Appear Before Men

Once upon a time angels of God appeared and mingled with human beings on earth. They had personal relationship with humans. The verses that testify this fact can be read in Genesis 6:1-4, " And it came to pass when men began to multiply on the face of the earth, and daughters of men that they were fair, and they took them wives of all which they chose. And the Lord said, My spirit shall not always strive with man, for that he also is flesh, yet his days shall be a hundred and twenty years.

There were giants in the earth in those days, and also after that, when the sons of God came in unto the daughters of men, and they bore children to them, the same became mighty men which were of old men of renown, and God saw the wickedness of man was great in the earth, and every imagination of the thoughts of his heart was only evil continually. And it repenteth the Lord that he had made man on the earth, and it grieved him at his heart.

We have known from these verses that angels or sons of God took with them daughters of men and bore children. Wickedness rapidly grew and the anger of the Lord drove him to destroy the human race in the face of the earth. Let us read Genesis 6:7, " And the Lord said, I will destroy man whom I have created from the face of the earth; both man, and beast, and the creeping thing, and the fowls of the air; for it repenteth me that have made them."

In the preceding discussions, we learned that angels or sons of God bore children with daughters of men. The growth of wickedry changed the face of the earth because God destroyed them. Despite the deluge that annihilated human beings to creeping things, the family of the righteous man, Noah and his family were saved by embarking into the ark. God made a covenant with Noah and commanded him to " be fruitful and multiply" In Genesis 9:1, " And God blessed Noah and his sons, and said unto them, Be fruitful and multiply, and replenish the earth."

Today, despite the population explosion particularly in the third world countries the growth of population continues that apparently bring poverty to more people. Nowadays, Shall we say to ourselves and to others to be fruitful and multiply ? No. It is not practical to multiply because of over population that causes distress, starvation, immorality and wickedry. Sometimes, man's reasoning is confusing and unacceptable because of wrong understanding and interpretation of the Word in the bible.

To those who do not understand the phrase they read, they will claim that it is a command to multiply. You will see the results; poverty, joblessness, vagrancy, and criminality. These are the factors that over population has brought to many poor nations. People have become aware of this problem that is why birth control measures have been formulated and contraceptives manufactured for prolific families.

There are people who believe they should multiply because it was commanded by God despite their difficulties in life. People should not be misled and misinterpreted the command of God. The question is, To whom God commanded to be fruitful and multiply ? Let us read the answer in Genesis 9:1, " And God blessed Noah and his sons, and said unto them. Be fruitful and multiply, and replenish the earth."

This verse is very clear that the command was given to Noah and not to the people of nowadays nor to the Gentiles. It was commanded to Noah to replenish the earth because of the aftermath of the deluge and mankind had to scatter anew the face of the earth to make dominion over all creatures. The command is not for today's generation because of the apparent and self-explanatory situation of people on earth now. We should realize the fact that God will not order that command to the wicked people because it will mean multiplication of wicked people also. Practically, multiplication is not to those bad and poor people but to those good and well off people.

Others may say, have we not the right to multiply? Nobody is holding you to multiply if you can. But it will multiply for the reason of having a big family but without means, well it's up to you to bear the burden. Economically and practical living dictate your decision in life. You will see its effect after all. This elaboration is for spiritual reasoning only.

There is really a big effect on men the lack of understanding and knowledge of the Word of God which is aggravated by nowadays false prophets who deceive and mislead many people. It follows that when the teachings are unrighteous, the works of the followers bear unrighteousness. The bible's instructions are not just taught to men but it need a lot of studies and understanding. We really have to scrutinize the Word that was said to read and study. It is not a question anymore; if we see and hear that many are misled and deceived. If these people are taught the right thing it follows that they do the right thing. It also follows that these effects are attributable to abusive teachers. A certain verse in Isaiah 56:11 says, " Yea, they are greedy dogs which can never have enough, and they are shepherds that cannot understand ; they all look to their own way, everyone for his gain from his quarter."The angels were the first celestial beings that were created by God. Job 38:4-7, " Where wast thou when I laid the foundations of the earth? ?Declare, if thou hast understanding. Who hath laid the measures thereof if thou knowest? Or who hath stretched the line upon it?

Whereupon are the foundations thereof fastened? Or who laid the corner some thereof; when the mornings stars sang together, and all the sons of God shouted for joy?" The angels know all things on earth. The angels of God watch human beings on their activities on earth and tell them to God. Let us read, Matthew 18:10, " Take heed that ye despise not one of these little ones; for I say unto you, That in heaven their angels do always behold the face of my Father which is in heaven."

The servants of God are being watched and guided by angels. Let us read Proverbs 34:7, "The angels of the Lord encampeth round about them that fear him, and delivereth them." Another verse in Hebrew 12:22, reads,"but ye are come unto mount Zion, and unto the city of the living God, the heavenly Jerusalem, and to an innumerable company of angels."As you may know the angels of God are the celestial beings that God allow to know everything on earth. They tell things and what transpired on earth and to human beings and everything to God. They are so powerful and were given that amazing power to make things happen on earth. However, their superiority over human beings on earth will be reduced to the same fate as the fate of the human beings during the judgment day.

The condemned angels who sinned will be thrown to hell. Do angels sin? Our perception of angels are heavenly beings which do not sin because they are in heaven, but the bible tells us that angels also sin. Let us read 2Peter 2:4, " For if God spared not the angels that sinned, but cast them down to hell," and delivered them into chains of darkness, to be reserved unto judgment."

Lucifer and the angels are also creations who will also be judged on the day of Judgment. They are also creations of God, like human beings on earth, only they are celestial beings. Let us read 1 Chronicles 29:11, " Thine, O Lord, is the greatness, and the power, and the glory, and the victory, and the majesty: for all that is in the heaven and in the earth is thine, thine is the kingdom, O Lord, and thou art exalted as head above all." In this verse, The greatness and power of Our Lord God is proclaimed above all.

Satan or Lucifer was a fallen angel because he rebelled against God. Let us read, Isaiah 14:12-14, " How art thou fallen from heaven, O Lucifer, son of the morning! How art thou cut down to the ground, which didst weaken the nations ! For thou hast said in thine heart, I will ascend into heaven, I will exalt my throne above the stars of God; I will ascend above the heights of the clouds; I will be like the Most High," This tells of the ambition of Lucifer to equal God in His glory which consequently, turned Lucifer into a falling star who was later named Satan who keeps sowing wickedness since the dawn of time.

An Angel Appears Before a Gentile

God is pleased to people who are naturally pure in heart and good in their doings. It is not only in the Old Testament that we could read about the angel's appearance before men. Let us read Acts 10:22, " And they said, Cornelius the centurion, a just man, and one that feareth God, and of good report among all the nation of the Jews, was warned from God by a holy angel to send for thee into his house, and to hear words of thee". Cornelius was an Italian centurion who feared God and was so helpful to the people that God saw his clean heart, thus a holy angel was sent to his house so he could hear the message of God.

In this instance, we can never judge nor accuse any person by reason of his sex, religion, affiliation, race or color but what counts most is his good deeds and heart. Remember that God searches the hearts of men. He hears the prayers of a righteous man. This proves that God does not only hear the prayers of His people because there also people who believe in God who are not yet in the flock.

An angel of God appeared before Cornelius who was a Gentile but a God-fearing man. In other words, the teaching of Christ applies in this situation that there are those who are not under the law that perform the law but there are those who are under the law who do not perform the law. These people who do the law but not under the law would have a great chance of being saved in the last day. But there are those under the law that would not be saved in the last day.

CHAPTER 11

The Church of God

What was the name of the first Church of God? Where did the first Church originate?

The first church that God established for his people must have its name and origin. There are many churches today that appear which we do not know if they are of God. It is a fact that different church denominations that appear today may it be large and small. Some were built and established only sometime in the 4th century AD to early 17th century AD, whereas the original Church that God in the bible was built more than 2,000 years old since the time of the Hebrews led by prophet Moses.

Biblically, when the Israelites under the leadership of Moses went out of the bondage from Egypt they traveled in the wilderness at the foot of Mt. Sinai. In this mountain, he received the Ten Commandments of God. The Patriarchs of Israel were the firstborn who received the first teachings and commandments of God. They were the first people who served the living God. Eventually, the first church or congregation was formed in the wilderness and was called "Church of the Firstborn". This consisted of the patriarchs of Israel who were called the firstborn of Israel. These firstborn were chosen and holy because they obeyed God's commandments given to Moses.

Let us read Hebrew 12:23. " To the general assembly and church of the firstborn which are written in heaven and to God that judge of all, and to the spirits of just men made perfect."

History and the bible tell us that Israel was the chosen nation of God and its people were called the first born . This is proven in Exodus 4:22," Then say to Pharaoh, this is what the Lord says; Israel is my firstborn son." In many events that took place in this nation, Israel went through many trials, sufferings and struggle to stand as a great nation of God. Despite being the chosen people, many of them turned away from their faith and disobeyed God.

God got angry but some remained obedient and faithful as they remained the chosen few. The chosen few traveled in the wilderness with God. Many times God's miracles were witnessed by these people which signified that He was really with them, and yet some of them became stubborn and turned away. They became idolaters, back sliders and unrepentant. But some of them scattered because of persecution. Eventually, they spread out and they grouped according to their beliefs and ways.

They scattered the earth. They were lost and isolated from the genuine and original congregation of the firstborn. Let us read, Romans 10 which reads," For they being ignorant of God's righteousness and going about to establish their own righteousness have not submitted themselves unto righteousness of God." This verse is a testimony for people who fall apart from the righteousness of God not to mention those who remained with God but were persecuted. In the days of Lord Jesus Christ, the Church of God was restored.

He preached to all nations, to Samaria, Judea and Galilea. He wanted to gather the lost flock of Israel. Jesus gathered His first disciples and preached the gospel of salvation. In this occasion, the lost Church of God (of the firstborn was restored) Paul, the apostle became the administrator of the church of God in different towns and cities in Israel.

The testimony of the bible that the church in which the disciples and apostles of Christ is the Church of God that can be read in 1Corinthians 4:2, " Unto the church of God which is at Corinth, to them that are sanctified in Christ Jesus, called to be saints, with all that in every place call upon the name of Jesus Christ our Lord, both theirs and ours;"

Another verse proving that the church is the church of God is in Acts 20:28, " Take heed therefore unto yourselves, and to all the flock, over the which the Holy Ghost hath made you overseers, to feed the church of God, which he hath purchased with his own blood." And other churches of God were established throughout Israel. Acts 9:31. " Then, had the churches rest throughout all Judea and Galilee and Samaria, and were edified; and walking in the fear of the Lord, and in the comfort of the Holy Ghost, were multiplied."

This church of God which was established in different parts of Israel in the past was lost because of persecution and scattered abroad until its revival in these last days in which its members would only cleave to be part of the church, as what the bible instructs in Roman 12:9. ' to cleave with which is good" All the members of the church of God should join the church , and obey the laws and teachings that are written in it.

Men are not expected to found their own churches, otherwise, they are false, but the instruction is to cleave with the Church of God which is good. Notice that there are many different churches bearing different names other than the Church of God today. Remember, there is only one Church of God that serves and worships God according to the bible today. This is the church that is appointed to teach the gospel of salvation in the last days.

The church of God is the church that opened up the mystery of the sealed book (bible) in these days when end time comes. (Daniel 12:4) The bible teaches us the existence of the Church of God as the church that Christ and the Apostle Paul taught in the bible to be the official name of the church. We can read the name of the church of God in 1Corinthians 1:1-2 that say," Paul, called to be an apostle of Christ Jesus by the will of God, and our brethren Sosthenes, To the church of God in Corinth, to those sanctified in Christ Jesus and called to be holy,". There are other verses in the bible that assert that the church of God is the name of the church where present-day Christians should cleave.

God's People From The East

The bible has told a prophecy that in the last days there will emerge people of God from the east who will be saved and will make the God of the bible their true and real God. These people are not people from Israel but the Gentiles from the east. It is clear in the verse of the bible in Zechariah 8:7, which says, " Thus saith the LORD of hosts, Behold, I will save my people from the east country, and from the west country; and I will bring them, and they shall dwell in the midst of Jerusalem; and they shall be my people and I will be their God, in truth and in righteousness." It is clear that a country and nation in the east where this group of people (church) will become God's people in the last day will serve God. These people which include the wise men will teach the gospel of salvation up to the ends of the earth that is, the west country or nation where those people who would believe will also be saved.

It should not be misinterpreted that a certain country located in the east is being referred here is not Israel although it is located in the east (east Asia minor or middle east) it was the first nation in the east that became the first nation to serve and worship God but in the end time a certain country in the east has been appointed to be His nation and that is revealed in Isaiah 24:14-15, which say, " They shall lift up their voice, they shall sing for the majesty of the LORD, they shall cry aloud from the sea. Wherefore glorify ye the LORD in the fires, even the name of the LORD God of Israel in the isles of the sea"

.

Take note the last phrase, " isles of the sea" that are being referred here are the islands of the sea. Which country in the east comprises a thousand islands of the seas? Could it be Japan, Malaysia, China, Singapore, Indonesia, Philippines? Try to check it out in the map the locations of these countries which possess a thousand islands in the east. Which nation is most likely to have those islands? It cannot be Japan, Malaysia, China, Singapore, Indonesia, Myanmar nor Laos and Vietnam because they do not have a hundred or thousand islands.

And yet, those countries or nations mentioned are not Christian nations where Christianity is a minority religion. It may be astonishing and surprising to know the truth that isles of the sea being referred to in the bible verse in the book of Isaiah is the Philippines because it has a thousand islands and that Christian religion is the most dominant religion in the country. See the rest of the countries in the east if they comprise a thousand islands.

The certainty that it is the Philippines is that no other Christian countries in the east believes God as the nation of the church of God that already exists nowadays. It cannot be the neighboring countries in the east because Japan has the most populous people who believe in Shintoism and Buddhism. China believes also in Buddhism that is a dominant religion there. Malaysia, Singapore, Indonesia, Vietnam and other neighboring countries believe in Buddhism, Mohammedanism or Islam much more of the people in India that have many religions where Christianity is a minority religion. The people in the Philippines are God-fearing people as they are very religious in character that when they are preached about Christianity they have the tendency to listen, respect and if convinced, may eventually accept what other preachers offer.

Although, the majority is a Catholic-Christian, there are numerous Christian congregations that exist in the archipelago. People welcome foreign teachers or evangelists coming from the different parts of the world bringing with them a faith called Christianity or fundamental Christianity. In other words, Christianity is a dominant religion in the country although people embrace Christian religion in different ways.

But only in the Philippines, there is the so-called church of God not founded by mere men but they cleaved to that which is good (Book of Romans 12:9) as instructed by God. They are the end time people that will receive the promise of God in which the fulfillment of the prophecy shall be absolute in the last day. However, the church of God is not alone in the Philippines but there are a number of churches of God; that are registered in the Securities and Exchange Commission representing the church.

Christians may be confused about this church because there are many claims about this church theirs is the genuine church that is in the bible that is why they use the name. But despite the many claims about the churches of God, we can still identify which of these churches is the one that has the standard that is required of by the bible.

The church of God that has cleaved to that which is good (Roman12:9) and not founded by men. The measurement is the teachings whether they are of God or not. Whether the church administrator is sent of God or not you will come to know when you hear and listen until you believe. That it is the church of God in the last days as prophesied by the bible.

Because Israel had become His people in the past but the promise and prophecy in this situation is located in the east where the bible attests and supports this allegation in 1Peter 2:10. " which in time past were not a people , but are now the people of God, which had not obtained mercy, but now have obtained mercy." It is not Israel that is being referred to in this verse because the Gentiles were not God's people in the past but, the Israelites or Hebrews first, and then in the end time the Gentiles will become His people who will be partakers in the promise of salvation as these wise Gentiles will preach and teach the gospel of Christ in many parts of the world particularly in the west where many will also be saved.

The wise people of the east will be the key people who will be given insight to understand and preach the sealed books of the bible and they will herald this understanding of the gospel to the people of the world. As they preach and teach in these last days many will be purified or cleansed and those who believe will be part of the church or group that will be saved in the end time. These groups did not established their church but they cleaved to that which is good and commanded in the bible.

To confirm that this group of people (believers) in the east will emerge to be the church of God that will be saved in the end time we must refer and know the answer or confirmation from the bible. 1 Peter 2:10 says, " which in time past were not a people but are now the people of God; which had not obtained mercy, but now have obtained mercy." We should think that in the past the Hebrews were the first people of God and not the Gentiles and this group of people in the east will only emerge in this 20th century or in the end time as prophesied in the book of Zechariah.

Take note that these wise people will emerge in the last days and that they will be the ones to understand and open the sealed books of the bible. Perhaps, we may ask, why ? Has the bible not understood and opened by various church-people in the past generation?

Yes. But not since the time of Christ and the Apostles. The bible says, many false prophets, false churches and false Christ will emerge on earth with different motives. They built their own churches for different motives as they even confess in their mouth about God but their hearts are full of inequities and superficiality. They will never understand the bible even if they interpret it in their own ways because they are not bound to receive the understanding of the sealed Word because of their filthy hearts and intention.

But the church of God that was built by Christ will be restored in the last day where the wise will understand and open up the seal of the bible. In other words, for many centuries since the time of

Christ and the Apostles the bible had been sealed nor understood by the generation of various congregations. Yes, because the church of God was not yet restored and that those wise men who would be appointed in the end time had not yet come. But now they have come, the bible has been opened and unsealed. This proves that we are already living in the last days prior to coming of Christ as what the bible tells.

To prove that the bible had been sealed nor understood in the past let us read Daniel 12:4 which says, " But thou, O Daniel, shut up the words, and seal the book, even to the time of the end: many shall run to and fro, and knowledge shall be increased." In Daniel 12:9, " And he said, Go thy way, Daniel; for the words are closed up and sealed till the time of the end."From that verse, we have already known that since the time of the prophet Daniel the bible was already shut out or sealed until the time of the end. Until the time of the end means that it will be opened and unsealed in the last days where the following events shall occur : where many shall run to and fro and knowledge shall be increased. Added to these occurrences are the succeeding verses in Daniel 12:10 which says, "

Many shall be purified, and made white, and tried; but the wicked shall do wickedly; and none of the wicked shall understand; but the wise shall understand;" The sealed book therefore will be opened and understood in the end time when knowledge shall be increased, many people will be purified, many shall run to and fro, the wicked shall do wickedly, and none of them shall understand, but the wise shall understand. The question is, in which era does these events are happening ?

Just observe and notice that these events are happening today. This is the last days or end time generation. How did I say that we are living in these events mentioned in those verses and that our time is the prophetic generation being referred to in the book of Daniel.

Just think about each event and we would come up with the conclusion that this is true and applicable to our time. First, knowledge shall be. increased.(Daniel 12:4). Apparently, almost all modern inventions, discoveries and successful and amazing explorations under water and space are being launched by men today. Modern technologies, weapons, robotics and computers have been manufactured.

Did all these things happen in the past. No. Only in this present time. Space has been explored by modern and advance spacecrafts. Fast moving and modern vehicles can transport people to different places in a short span of time. Knowledge of men has really increased when modern methods in finances were introduced, such as the e-card replacing money to obtain cash from the ATM(automated teller machine) buying goods using this e-card or credit card can make transactions easy and fast when no cash is available, hence, safer than to show and bring money in the pocket.

Laser machine is now used in surgery to remove gall stones inside the human body as it can also perform eye surgery to remove cataract in the human eyes. Production of robots in manufacturing and assembly plants that almost reduced and displaced manpower has been employed as many superpowers are manufacturing fatal weapons for mass destruction including chemical and biological weapons. Nuclear weapon might be the ultimate destructive discovery of mankind in this instance of advance knowledge of man.

Unlike in the past centuries, man started from the spears and swords, then powder guns and eventually in the 19th,and 20th century since the industrial revolution a rapid technological transformation occurred particularly from the west where flying machines were developed until the 21st century more amazing discoveries, inventions and developments have taken place. These are the manifestations of the increasing knowledge of men that is stated in the verse of the bible.

Second, when the wise people of God understood the gospel of salvation, many were cleansed and will be cleansed or purified. Notice that in this present dispensation, when people believe the gospel and get baptized they turn away from their wicked ways, such as fornications, idolatry, stealing or robbing, and other forms of filthiness.

People seek the truth through the gospel and teachings of the wise men of the appointed time. Although, nowadays many false churches and false prophets appear and yet the teachings of the wise men in the last days will persist and save many. Third, the wicked or evil men will continue to do wickedry according to the verse in the book of Daniel while many are purified.

This the present scenario which we can see, read and hear in the news in the tv, print media, and radio almost every day. Almost every day these media show brutal killings, murders, massacres, robbery, arson, cruelty and other wickedry of men are happening today. The situation is much worse than in the past where today wicked men take drugs to aggravate wickedry.

Fourth, the sealed books of the bible will be opened in the last day. While it was closed before, the wise men and people of God in the east have cleaved to that church of God, learned and understood the words in the bible. Therefore, the church of God that was lost in the past has been restored and now preaching the word to many nations.

No churches in this generation nor in the past have opened up and understood the words but in this era when the end is at the threshold; and when the signs and indications that are stated in the bible are being fulfilled. This is the church of God in the east, the fulfillment of the prophecy that one church that has opened the sealed book of mystery in the last days.

The End Time People

Prophecy of Ezekiel

The prophet Ezekiel tells of the house or church (1Timothy 3:15) where God shall dwell and stay forever in the last day. Does God dwell in the house or church, a building structure or temple made by man's hands? Definitely No. Ezekiel 43:3-5 attest to this fact. What is being referred to in the vision of Ezekiel ? It is not a literal house or church structure as we all see and know but it is the church people which are the temple of God.

The verse states that there is the church people in the east. Take note the place in the east, that is being emphasized in this verse. Ezekiel 43:7 says, " It is revealed that God will dwell in this church in the midst of Israel forever." The church that is being referred to in the verse is the " people" or "members" of the congregation. So, it is not Israel nor its people that would be made His last dwelling place.

As we all know in biblical history, Israel, the first born who served God was the first people that served and worshipped God. They were the chosen people in the old testament times but then, after disobedience and transgressions God has already changed history and turned away from them.

The prophecy in the last day states that there is a new church (people) with whom God will dwell and save in the last day and forever that is located in the east. Since Israel is located in the middle east it is not the one being pointed out in this prophecy but the one that is located in the east, that is somewhere in the far east, the nation located on that country will become his people in the last day.

This church of God as prophesied to emerge in the last days is now existing and has been prophesying the gospel of salvation in many parts of the world including the west, north and south where, according to the prophecy will also save the people in the many parts of the world. (See for yourself, which country and nation in the east is now bearing the name of the church of God that preaches the gospel in accordance with the righteousness in the bible) Although there are many bogus churches of God that appear today, we may only identify which the church of God by their teachings and obedience to the law of Christ in the bible.

The question is, who are these people of God in the east? They are the Gentiles who cleaved with which is good (Church of God; Romans 12:9) They received the promise of salvation reserved for them by Christ.

As promised, the Gentiles are partakers in spiritual things. Romans 15:27 says, "It hath pleased them verily; and their debtors they are. For if the Gentiles have been made partakers of spiritual things, their duty is also to minister unto them in carnal things." Although, originally not people of God, gentiles have become partakers of spiritual things or have become parts of spiritual things that God has prepared. In the same way, that gentiles are duty bound to minister what they have partaken.

Another supporting verse that Gentiles have become people of God is in Ephesians 2: 11-14, which say, " Wherefore remember, that ye being in time past Gentiles in the flesh, who are called un circumcision by that which is called Circumcision in the flesh made by hands; that at that time ye were without Christ, being aliens from the commonwealth of Israel, and strangers from the covenants of promise, having no hope, and without God in the world.

But now, in Christ Jesus, ye who sometime were far off are made nigh by the blood of Christ. For he is our peace, who hath made both one, and hath broken down the middle wall of partition between us:" Therefore, with these verse, Gentiles and the Israelites have no more distinction when it comes to salvation, because Gentiles have become God's people through Christ Jesus whose blood had become a redemption for our sins. To those who will listen to his words now, and have faith in Him will be become his people.

The Chosen People of God

In what ways may God talk to Gentiles nowadays ? Why Gentiles ? Are not the Israelites, His chosen people whom we know

God spoke only ? Since Israel was His firstborn and His chosen people in the past, God has sent his Son to save the Gentiles, and became also his people through His teachings and the teachings of the prophets and disciples. However, nowadays, the Jews or Jewish nation is no longer the chosen people of God.

The events in the past became the reason why the Jews why they had been abandoned by God and turned away from them. As first people of God they became disobedient and they practiced all forms of wickedry that were abominable in God's sight.

In the bible there are many recorded events that the nation of Israel had committed that caused God to get angry, thus, they suffered the consequences of their sins. They were punished they passed through many trials and difficulties since then towards the present time. Others remained faithful but others went their way. The world has become a witness for generations about their journey on earth, their struggle, endeavor, success, and wars. Despite their being persecuted God still protects them and the love of God can still be felt by them when Israel became independent in 1948.

Many Jews who scattered in many parts of the world returned to settle down. The most unforgettable and horrible memory of the Jews in modern time is the Holocaust that happened during World War II. It was prophesied that Israel would be destroyed and its people would suffer in the hands of enemies. One enemy that was Anti-Semitic was Hitler, a gentile who hated the Jews so much that he ordered the annihilation of more than 6 million Jews .

It was a clear persecution of the nation of Israel who first served the living God. History will never forget the scar left on this nation that were persecuted and put to shame and death. However, today, Israel as an independent nation has been restored. A powerful and progressive country. We still believe that the hand of God is still with them that leads them to freedom and restoration despite the many wars and issues they are facing.

Today, while we already believe that the fallen or lost church of God has been restored for the present people of God now in East, the teachings of the gospel continues until the coming of Christ. As promised, the Gentiles are partakers in spiritual things. Romans 15:27 says, "It hath pleased them verily; and their debtors they are.

For if the Gentiles have been made partakers of spiritual things, their duty is also to minister unto them in carnal things." Although, originally not people of God, gentiles have become partakers of spiritual things or have become parts of spiritual things that God has prepared. In the same way, that gentiles are duty bound to minister what they have partaken.

Another supporting verse that Gentiles have become people of God is in Ephesians 2: 11-14, which say, " Wherefore remember, that ye being in time past Gentiles in the flesh, who are called un circumcision by that which is called Circumcision in the flesh made by hands; that at that time ye were without Christ, being aliens from the commonwealth of Israel, and strangers from the covenants of promise, having no hope, and without God in the world.

But now, in Christ Jesus, ye who sometime were far off are made nigh by the blood of Christ. For he is our peace, who hath made both one, and hath broken down the middle wall of partition between us:" Therefore, with these verses, Gentiles and the Israelites have no more distinction when it comes to salvation, because Gentiles have become God's people through Christ Jesus whose blood had become a redemption for our sins.

To those who will listen to his words now, and have faith in Him will be become his people. After those times mentioned in the bible where God communicated through His prophets, and through the Son, and disciples, in what way does God in the present dispensation speak to His people? John 14:26, says, "But the Comforter, which is the Holy Ghost, whom the Father will send in my name, he shall teach you all things, and bring all things to your remembrance, whatsoever I have said unto you."

Therefore, nowadays, God has sent the Comforter which is the Holy Ghost to teach all things and bring all things to the remembrance of his people. That is why there are true believers nowadays whom the Comforter (Holy Ghost) guides to speak the word of God to the people. Notice with amazement that these chosen messengers speak the word from the bible without looking and tracing the lines and verses from the bible as the people ask questions to him. These people are led by the Holy Ghost and the words they speak are truly and directly derived from the bible. He can deliver the word infallibly but accurately as asked by the listeners. Does God speak to people nowadays ? Is He still communicating with people today ?

How does God speak to people nowadays? The bible tells us that God still speaks to people as in the past, in Hebrew 1:1-2, " God, who at sundry times and in divers manners spake in time past unto the fathers by the prophets, hath in these last days spoken unto us by his Son, when he hath appointed heir of all things by whom also he made the worlds."These verses confirm that in different times in the past God spoke to Patriarchs through His prophets, and in the last days also have spoken to us through his Son, Jesus Christ.

Therefore, Prophets were the medium by which the messages of God to his people was being transmitted. Messages were known to prophets by a dream and the latter heralded the messages to the people. This is proven in Numbers 12:16 which says, " And he said, Hear now my words: If there be a prophet among you, I the Lord will make myself known unto him in a dream."

God Talks To His People Today

Who are the people with whom God talks today? We should realize that God does not communicate audibly to any church leader nor Has God speak to any man nowadays. There are many teachers of faith nowadays who claim that God is communicating with them as they relay the messages to their followers. With whom God talks and who are these people with whom He talks with? The bible tells in Revelation 2:29 says, " He that hath an ear, let him hear what the Spirit saith unto the churches."

Do all people have ears to enable them hear and understand the message of God? The message of God is in the bible. Do all people understand what they read in the bible? Not all people will understand even if they read the bible verbatim because God gives an ear to those righteous and upright people who have the desire to seek God in the hearts. God knows what's in our hearts and He knows his true people. There is a reader of the word in the bible that everyone should listen. He gives them ears to hear and understanding to understand as the reader reads the word from the bible.

Proverbs 20:12 says, " The hearing ear, and the seeing eye, the LORD hath made even both of them." Therefore, those people whom God has given ears should listen as the word the word is being read and understanding will come, thereby, knowing the will of God. The Holy Ghost will guide his people and make them remember the words that were read.

This is attested in Revelation 1:3, which says, " Blessed is he that readeth, and they that hear the words of this prophecy, and keep those things which are written therein; for the time is at hand." But those false prophets and followers nowadays will not be able to hear nor understand nor see the will of God even if they read the whole bible, instead they will be misled and imperiled by the false teachings by their false teachings.

They are those being referred by the bible as the blind who are leading the blind that will fall into the pit. This is proven in Matthew 15:14 which says, " Let them alone; they be blind leaders of the blind. And if the blind lead the blind, both shall fall into the ditch."The difference between people who listen to the one reading the words of God in the bible from those who do not?

There must be a reader of the words of God in the bible as there are listeners to the one reading them. Thus, by hearing the words of God, faith will come out of the listeners. Where does faith and belief come? It is from listening to the one who is reading the words of God. Romans 10:17 says, " So then faith cometh by hearing, and hearing by the word of God."

So, therefore, it is really necessary that we listen to the words of God when being read in the bible by the reader, then faith within us will come that will make us believe and accept God and Jesus Christ as our Saviors. Once again, the knowledge of the mystery of the kingdom of God is given to his disciples as in the past. Those who have been given eyes will be able to see and hearing will hear and understand the words of God. Unless those who have not been able to hear, see and understand should repent first and listen to the words of God in order to hear, see and understand the words of God.

This is attested in Mark 4:10-12 which say, " And when he was alone, they that were about him with the twelve asked of him the parable. And he said unto them, Unto you it is given to know the mystery of the kingdom, all these things are done in parables: that seeing they may see, and not perceive; and hearing they may hear, and not understand; lest at any time they should be converted, and their sins should be forgiven them."

In the Old Testament time, when the people wanted to know the message of God to them they would go to the seer or prophet and ask him. This is what the bible tells in I Samuel 9:9, "(Beforetime in Israel, when a man went to inquire of God, thus he spake, Come, and let us go to the seer: for he that is now called a Prophet was beforetime called a Seer.) In the present day, as mentioned earlier the Comforter or the Holy Ghost will make us remember all things when we read the words of God in the bible by the reader.

Therefore, it is necessary that a true believer reads the bible in order to know the things of God. The bible is the only source of spiritual knowledge where we can rely for salvation and to know what is coming to us.

However, as mentioned earlier, those who cannot see, hear and understand the words in the bible, they would apparently display their bibles in their tables, bookshelves, and sometimes put it on top of their altar being enlightened by candles.

This is indeed a fact because the bible says, in 1Corinthians 4:9, " For I think that God hath set forth us the apostles last, as it were appointed to death; for we are made a spectacle unto the world, and to angels, and to men." Apparently, there are pictures, monuments and carvings on the walls which depict in men's interpretations, the apostles and the inscriptions in marble stones the words derived from the bible that have become spectacles for men and attraction for others signifying the piety of those who people who have been blinded by their false beliefs.

CHAPTER 12

The Dwelling Place of Evil Spirits

It you have something to ask and reason out the Lord says, in Isaiah 1:18 " Come now, and let us reason together, saith the LORD; though your sins be as scarlet, they shall be as white as snow; though they be red like crimson, they shall be as wool" While we battle and defend our faith against adversaries with their false teachings and prophets we should know that the disciples did not use weapons nor their hands in defending their faith in Christ, but by the spirit.

Our struggle is not against the body or physical being of our adversaries but the spirits that are dwell in them. Ephesians 6:12 says, " For wrestle not against flesh and blood, but against principalities, against powers, against the rulers of the darkness of this world, against spiritual wickedness in high places."

The powers of darkness are dwelling those wicked men and false prophets and workers that deceive many. Thus, our struggle against them is not by flesh and blood but by spirit. Those are the spiritual evils that drive them to do wickedry and disseminate false teachings as they do evil works. Evil men are being used by these evil spirit being which dwell in high places of the clouds or in lower level of the heavens. They could be in the first heaven.

You may ask , do evil spirits live in heaven? Yes they dwell in the first heaven which according to the Ephesians 6:12 " "....spiritual wickedness in <u>high places</u>." Why did I say in high places? Because Satan was going up there or coming to and fro in earth . In Job 1:7, " And the LORD said unto Satan, Whence comest though? Then Satan answered the LORD, and said, From going to and fro in earth, and from walking up and down in it." Therefore, when Satan was asked by the LORD where had he been during that time he was in heaven also, but only in the first heaven.

We should know that there are three heavens, and God and His Son Jesus Christ are in third heaven which is called by the bible as Paradise. The proof can be read in 2Corinthians 12:2 " I knew a man in Christ above fourteen years ago, (whether in the body, I cannot tell; or whether out of the body, I cannot tell; God knoweth) how that he was caught up into paradise"

Who is this man taken to paradise? He was the apostle Paul. He was not taken to heaven in physical form but in spirit. His spirit was caught up into paradise to witness and learn many things that are not present in the physical world. When he returned to earth he could not utter what he had experience but what he knew was a very heavenly experience that no man is not allowed to utter on earth.

Spirits that Dwell into Human Beings

Spiritually clean Christians are dwelt by the spirit of God. Did you know that your body is the temple of the Spirit of God? This is asserted in 1Corinthians 3:126, " Know ye not that ye are the temple of God, and that the Spirit of God dwelleth in you? Therefore, these Christians produce good works since they are dwelt with the spirit of God. Quality Christians bear fruits in the spirit. Let us read Galatians 5:22, " But the fruit of the Spirit is love, joy, love, peace, long-suffering, gentleness, goodness, faith."

How about those Christians and unbelievers who do not have the spirit of God? What kind of spirits do they have? Those human beings that do not have the spirit of God walk in the flesh. And the works of the flesh manifest in them. This is what Galatians 5:19-21 speaks of, " Now the works of the flesh are manifest, which are these, adultery, fornication, uncleanness, lasciviousness, idolatry, witchcraft, hatred, variance, emulations, wrath, strife, murders, drunkenness, reveling, and such like: of the which I tell you before, As I have also told you in time past, that they which do such things shall not inherit the kingdom of God."

Therefore, if you are a Christian struggling against the works of the flesh as stated in the previous verses, try to resist the evil works of flesh and submit to God so that you life may be pleasing to God. Let us read James 4: 7-8, " Submit yourselves therefore to God, Resist the devil, and he will flee from you. Draw nigh to God, and he will draw nigh to you. Cleanse your hands, ye sinners; and purify your hearts, ye double-minded."

The Imprisoned Spirits Beneath the Earth

On the other hand, the body of a dead one will rest to the soil while the spirit will return to God. This is asserted in Job 12:10 " in his hands is the life of every creature and the breath of all mankind." Where does the spirit of a dead man go? In the hands of God as the verse says. It may mean that the spirits that go back to go is already under the disposition of God. That is what we do not know where but only literally into the hands of God. The bible reveals that Jesus Christ died on the cross and buried for three days, he went down to the depths of the earth to preach or proclaim his victory over death to the wicked spirits which were imprisoned there.

Let us read I Peter 3:19, " by which also he went and preached(proclaimed) unto the spirits in prison;" Who were these wicked spirits who had been in captivity into the depths of the earth? In the Old Testament, these wicked spirits were the angels who took and mutated with human beings for themselves . They were the angels assigned in their respective assignments to guard or watch but they became wicked and disobedient to God. The offspring of these angels with human beings were abnormally giants in their physical appearance during that time.

These spirits were already condemned to be punished in the last day as what the bible teaches in 2Peter 2:4, " For if God spared not the angels that sinned, but cast them down to hell," and delivered them into chains of darkness, to be reserved unto judgment;" However, angels are bestowed with astounding power and knowledge as they know all things on earth. This is what the bible tells in 2Samuel 14:20,"to fetch about this form of speech hath thy servant Joab done this thing; and my lord is wise, according to the wisdom of an angel of God, to know all things that are in the earth." But angels will also be subjected to judgment by the saints in the last day.

The Spirit-Angels

If men were sent by God to save other men, then, it is also the same that angels are being sent to serve all men of God. Angels are spirit – beings that cannot be seen by our naked eyes. Angels are called " ministering spirits" by the bible. In Hebrew 1:14 says, " Are they not all ministering spirits, sent forth to minister for them who shall be heirs of salvation?" In the said verse, it is said that angels are ministering spirits sent to save the people of God. They Spirit-angels that guard people of God. Why is it said that angels are ministering spirits sent to save the people of God. Why is it that these spirits are sent to minister and serve only those who are not God's people. Are Gentiles not given ministering spirits ? People of God are righteous and have fear of God which angels protect and guard wherever they go.

The wicked men do not have Guardian spirit-angels because they have nothing to lose and worth protecting for. In fact, they are vile and filthy people. The reason that guardian spirits are protecting the righteous ones is to keep them away from sinning and wickedry. Let us read the verse that says about the works of ministering spirits, In Psalms 34:7, " *The angels of the Lord encampeth round about them that fear him and delivereth them.*"In other words, angels of God play an important role in the salvation of men although they are spirit beings. Even Jesus Christ at the time when he was being tempted by the devil was surrounded and supported by angels of God. In Matthew 4:5-6 read, " Then the devil taketh him up into the holy city, and sitteth him in a pinnacle of the temple, and hath unto him. If thou be the Son of God, cast thyself down; for it is written, he shall give his angels charge concerning thee; and in their hands thy shall bear thee up, list at any time thou dash they foot against a stone."

God himself sent these angels for his servants in the event of danger. Even during the time of Moses, an angel of the Lord was sent to serve them. Let us read the verse in Exodus 23:20, " Behold, I send an angel before thee, to keep thee in the way, and to bring three into the place which I have prepared. If angels are sent to serve God's people, we should know that not all angels are sent by God because there are angels or spirits sent by the devil. These are the spirits that follow Satan to deceive people. Let us read this testimony to see the origin of these spirits of the devil. In Revelations 12:7-9, " And there was war in heaven; Michael and his angels fought against the dragon and the dragon fought and his angels, and prevailed not; neither was their place found any more in heaven. And the great dragon was cast out that old serpent called the devil, and Satan which deceiveth the whole world; he was cast out into the earth, and his angels were cast out with him.

As we have said earlier, wicked men do not have guardian angels by reason that these men are being pushed by evil spirits to do wickedry. In a revelation about angels, the prophet John received revelations and visions from God through an angel. We can read this testimony in Revelation 22:8, " And I, John saw these things, and heard them and when I had heard and seen, I fell down to worship before the feet of the angel which showed me these things."In this verse John thought that he was speaking with God, that is why he fell down and worship before the angel but he was refrained from bowing before an angel because it is God with whom all men shall bow down.

In a certain verse in Revelation 1:1, " The revelation of Jesus Christ which God gave unto him to show unto his servants things which must shortly come to pass, and he sent and signified it by his angel unto his servant John."

CHAPTER 13

Aftermath of the Great Deluge

We have learned that something is impossible with God. At this point, we will mention that there were times when God repented , not repentance as what human beings are sorry for , but a compassion to save mankind from second in the lake of burning sulfur because of their wicked ways. God saved them to stop their vile ways, that is why the human race was wiped out in the face of the earth by the great deluge. In Genesis 9:11 reads, " and I will establish my covenant with you, neither shall all flesh be cut off any more by the waters of a flood: neither shall there anymore be a flood to destroy the earth." God wanted this deluge to happens because of the great sins of men. Wicked men must have to be eliminated and renew the race of mankind on earth.

Remember God is compassionate, He knows man's heart and emotion. His compassion was also shown He nearly destroyed Nineveh had the people turned from their wicked ways and repented. He sent Jonah to warn the people of Nineveh about the disaster that would come in the city. Let us read Jonah 3:10, " and God saw their works that they turned from their evil ways; and God repented of the evil, that he had said that he would do unto them, and he did it not."

The term "repent" does not mean that God repented because He made a mistake like human beings, No. Repent signifies sympathy or pathetic to human beings due to destruction they would suffer brought by their stubbornness and hardened hearts. God wanted them to be saved from hell. Another verse can be read with the same assertion that God repented with compassion. In Joel 12:13, reads," and rend your heart and not your garments and turn unto the Lord your God; for he is gracious and merciful, slow to anger, and of great kindness and repenteth him of the devil." For clarification the term used is, " relent in Jonah 3:9 (NIV), instead of repent, but in King James version, the term used is " repent"

Another verse in the bible which shows that God repented and grieved over the wickedness of men on earth is found in Genesis 6:5-6, " And God saw that the wickedness of man was great in the earth, and that every imagination of the thoughts of his heart was only evil continually. And it repented the Lord that he had made man on the earth, and it grieved him at his heart." Does repentance show that God made a mistake ?

Of course, Not. We all know that God is God. He is the creator of everything. He is a righteous and infallible God. Repent is compassion and sympathy to human destruction. He has all the reason to send destruction to wicked people. In the meantime, God knows the heart of man. He knows the good and evils in the hearts of men as he also knows their minds. God searches the hearts of men , 1 Chronicles 28:9 " And thou, Solomon my son, know thou the God of thy father, and serve him with a perfect heart and with a willing mind; for the Lord searcheth all hearts."

The thing that God does not know nor make interference is the decision and choice of men. The decision of men to choose right and wrong. Whether men will decide to do good or to do wrong. Remember that God gave men the free will to choose which one does he wants ;life or death

The book of Deuteronomy 30: 19, " I call heaven and earth to record this day against you, that I have set before you life and death, blessing and cursing,; therefore choose like, that both thou and thy seed may life." This verse affirms the choice between life and death whichever man wants. Take note that men have freedom or liberty. This liberty gives men the choice between good and evil. Therefore, God is also an advocate of freedom.

The Scourge in the Last Day

Mankind was destroyed during the great deluge on earth. It was a great flood that killed every tiny creature from creeping things to human beings which left nothing but Noah's family and a variety of species of animals which were embarked into the ark. However, God, after seeing this deluge and outcome of the great flood promised that He would not punish mankind again with the same type of punishment. What kind of punishment awaits mankind in the future? Will there be another Noah who will be saved ? What is it like in the last day on earth? When and how it shall happen? The bible says, earth's destruction will be like in the days of Noah when people were marrying, drinking, eating and building houses when suddenly the wrath of God which was the great flood came. Everybody was trapped and surprised and then came upon them their bitter end. So it is also the same when everybody is doing the same thing when the scourge of heaven shall come. And after the "Catching Up" in the air has taken place it would be followed by the raising of the dead in Christ first and then the living faithful whose bodies shall be transformed into heavenly bodies shall meet the Lord in the clouds, (1Corinthians 15:52, " In a moment in the twinkling of an eye, at the last trump, for the trumpet shall sound, and the dead shall be raised incorruptible, and we shall be changed, for this corruptible must put on incorruption, and this mortal must put on immortality").

The coming of the Lord in the clouds shall be accompanied by the voice of archangel with the trumpet of God. (1Thessalonians 4: 16-11 " For the Lord himself shall descend from heaven with a shout, with the voice of the archangel, and with the trump of God; and the dead in Christ shall rise first; then we which are alive and remain shall be caught up together with them in the clouds, to meet the Lord in the air: and so shall we ever be with the Lord" ,

Then after a thousand years reign of Christ on earth is over ,another one thousand years shall pass and the second resurrection shall take place for the dead without Christ to face the judgment seat of God. And after that event, earth shall be destroyed by fire and every living thing that creeps to a living flesh, soft and hard objects and all works of man will be burned to ashes and even the very hard object like steel and iron shall melt and everything shall disappear.

Thus, 2Peter 3 :10-12, " But the day of the Lord will come as a thief in the night; in the which the heavens shall pass away with a great noise, and the elements shall melt with fervent heat, the earth also and the works that are therein shall be burned up. Seeing, what manner of persons ought ye to be in all holy conversation and godliness, looking for and hasting unto the coming of the day of God, wherein the heavens being on fire shall melt with fervent heat " It means that even the hard object which is the metal or steel will melt because of the extreme heat on earth. And even the heavens being on fire shall melt on that day of the Lord God. According to the bible heaven and earth shall pass away but my world shall never pass away.

When God Is Angry

When Is God Angry ? How do we know if He is angry? God is angry to those who always disobey His commandments and do evil. Here on earth, many countries and parts of the world are shaken because of earthquake. When we are shaken by earthquake do not just think that it's just a natural cause or geological reasons such as movement of mountains of rocks under the earth; and movements of earth's crust that create slopes that move boulders of rocks toward the earth, but we should know that it is one way on how God expresses His anger.

Do you know that God is angry everyday because man unceasingly perform evil things? *Psalms 7:11 says, " God judgeth the righteous, and God is angry with the wicked every day."* And God is the one making the pillars of the earth to shake. Let us read *Job 9:5-6 " which removeth the mountains, and they know not; which overturneth them in his anger; which shaketh the earth out of her place, and the pillars thereof tremble."*

It is not only earthquake that God makes earth to tremble because of man's inequities and many sins but He also brings tsunami from the waters of the earth that cause destruction and death to man. *Amos 9:6 says, "It is he that buildeth his stories in the heaven, and hath calleth for the waters of the sea, and poureth them out upon the face of the earth: The LORD is his name." Therefore, we do not wonder why such natural calamities occur everywhere on the face of the earth. It is because man keeps evil works and wickedry that provoke God to cause all these things to happen.*

The bible tells us sinners not to continue in wicked ways nor stealing nor robbing but rather work with your hands or labor so you may be able to give something in need. *Ephesians 4:28 tells, " Let him that stole steal no more; but rather let him labor, working with his hands that thing which is good, that he may have to give to him that needeth."* Despite all those consequences mentioned in the previous issues, God also rejoices. And if you believe that, let us read Proverb 8:31, " God is rejoicing in the habitable part of his earth." In this verse, take note that God has his own earth. It is where

He lives even before the creation of the universe and the world we live in. Man should understand those verses in *Matthew 5:29-30, which says " And if they right eye offend thee, pluck it out, and cast it from thee; for it is profitable for thee that one of their members should perish, and not that thy whole body should be cast into hell. And if thy right hand offend thee, cut it off, and cast it from thee; for it is profitable for thee that one of their members should perish, and not that thy whole body should be cast into hell."*, should not be interpreted literally because when pluck out the eyes that sin you will die, how then can you change your life for the better?

You should interpret it spiritually, try not to make your eyes see lewd and sinful scenes; while you don't cut off your hand when you stole because you can no longer work with your hands and make your living but instead change for the better and avoid stealing. Those things should be interpreted spiritually and there are those verses in the bible that should be interpreted literally.

The bible teaches us that we should not submit ourselves to sins or its sinful nature. *Romans 6:12-13 say " Let not sin therefore reign in your mortal body, that ye should obey it in the lusts thereof. Neither yield ye your members as instruments of unrighteousness unto sin; but yield yourselves unto God, as those that are alive from the dead, and your members as instruments of righteousness unto God."*

CHAPTER 14

The Signs of the End time

Remember that the prophecy also tells the emergence of false prophets who teach different doctrines and will deceive many. The prophecy is happening today . The false prophets and false Christ have gone out of this world already professing themselves to many that they are sent. They even say they are the Christ. This prophecy is true and had been prophesied more than 2000 years ago in the book of *Matthew 24:24* which says, " *For there shall arise false Christ and false prophets and shall show great signs and wonders."*

Who do you know and which church do these signs and wonders happen? Their leader would even claim that he can raise the dead? Make cripple walk? Make blind see? Touch and hold serpents? These are signs and wonders that nowadays, false prophets and preachers will perform in public and inside their congregations.

While we mentioned in *1 Thessalonians 4:16, Matthew 24:27, Ephesians 4:19,* those significant events that will take place before the coming of Christ. The bible tells us and prophesies the time of Christ's coming.. *in Matthew 24:6-8 which say, " And ye shall hear of wars and rumors of wars: see that ye be not troubled; for all these things must come to pass, but the end is not yet. For nation shall rise against nation and kingdom against kingdom; and there shall be famines , and pestilences, and earthquakes, in divers places. All these are the beginning of sorrows."*

We should realize that these events prophesied more than 2000 years ago are already happening now. You cannot deny the wars that happened in many parts of the world in the past centuries and in the 20th and 21st centuries. For example : the Vietnam War; Afghanistan war; Iran-Iraq war; Kuwait or Persian Gulf War;

Kuwait Invasion by Iraq; African War in Somalia and other countries there; and now the Russian war with its Federate State of Georgia; and other wars in many parts of the world. Some wars might already ended but other wars are still on- going as there are unpredictable wars to erupt in other parts of the world. How many disasters have happened in the past and in this present Christian dispensation ? There are several disastrous wars and natural calamities like earthquakes that killed many in China; in Japan and in other parts of the world; volcanic eruptions in the Philippines, Italy, US, etc.; famines & pestilences in Africa and other parts of the world. The growing cases of deadly viruses that have killed many people everywhere in the world.

Records of human rights violations which are signs of man's coherence to evil and hatred in many countries are rampant. Persecution and senseless killings. Many have been deprived of their civilian rights, and rights to living and liberty. Have not all these things coincide with what the bible tells in *Matthew 14: 3-8* " *And as he sat upon the mount of Olives, the disciples came unto him privately, saying, Tell us, when shall these things be? And what shall be the sign of thy coming, and of the end of the world? And Jesus answered and said unto them? Take heed that no man deceive many. And ye shall hear of wars and rumors of wars; see that ye be not troubled; for all these things must come to pass, but the end is not yet. For nation shall rise against nation, and kingdom against kingdom; and there shall be famines and pestilences, and earthquakes, in divers places. All these are the beginning of sorrows."*

Therefore, these events are real and apparently happening now in our present dispensation. These are the signs prophesied by Christ in the book of Matthew. Take note of these signs because they are happening anywhere in many countries of the world now. They are the very signs stated in the bible and prophesied by our Lord Jesus Christ to his disciples and early Christians more than 2000 years ago.

But accordingly, these are just the beginning of sorrows, meaning to say that these sufferings and tribulations that we are experiencing today are just prelude to the great tribulation the bible is prophesying us. That one Great tribulation we shall experience is a prelude to the coming of Christ.

And there shall be signs in the sun[1], and in the moon, and in the stars[2]; and upon the earth distress of nations, with perplexity; the sea and the waves roaring; Men's hearts failing them for fear, and for looking after those things which are coming on the earth: for the powers of heaven shall be shaken." (Luke 21:25-26)" Signs have been occurring one after the other, people are truly afraid, and the governments and politicians are at a loss on what to do about all of these problems. Yet at the same time multitudes are saying that everything has gone on as it always has."

Knowing the Signs of the Last Days

> The significant events preceded by the coming of Christ are signs discussed above shall likewise be also when determining whether our generation is already in the last days. We may be able to know that we are already in the last days by reading and understanding the prophecies in the bible. What are the signs that we are already in the last days? The last days will be like those days of Noah; (Luke 17:27) " They did eat, they drank, they married wives, they were given in marriage, until the day that Noah entered into the ark, and the flood came, and destroyed them all."
>
> Take note of what is happening around you, aren't these things happening? But when punishment came, it would not be by flood anymore, but by fire. (2 Peter 3:10-12)

1. http://www.bibleprophecytruth.com/JesusChrist/thedarkday.asp
2. http://www.bibleprophecytruth.com/JesusChrist/shootingstars.asp

"But the day of the Lord will come as a thief in the night; in the which the heavens shall pass away with a great noise and the elements shall melt with fervent heat, the earth also and the works that are therein shall be burned up. Seeing then that all these things shall be dissolved, what manner of persons ought yet to be in all holy conversation and godliness, looking for and hasting unto the coming of the day of God, wherein the heavens being on fire shall be dissolved, and the elements shall melt with fervent heat?" In other words, fire will destroy things on earth on that day. The elects and chosen ones (Christians) will be able to understand the Word in the bible, that is, the prophecies and the parables that cannot be understood by man will be learned by wise men to prophesy.

Many shall be cleansed or purified in the last days because many will be able to hear and listen to the Word of God. (Daniel 12:9-10), " And he said, Go thy way Daniel; for the words are closed up and sealed till the time of the end. Many shall be purified, and made white, and tried; but wicked shall do wickedly; and none of the wicked shall understand; but the wise shall understand."

The original teachings of Christ to the Disciples and early Christians that were lost, set aside, and ignored by men will be found and taught again nowadays by the wise. Did you know that the original teachings were lost after the early Christians and disciples? But nowadays, it has been found by the wise men in the Church of God. (Jeremiah 6:16) " Thus saith the Lord, Stand ye in the ways, and see, and ask for the <u>old paths</u>, where is the good way, and walk therein, and ye shall find rest for your souls." The old paths being pointed here are the teachings from the true church of God where mankind is ordered to find for and follow. The lost and original teachings have been found in this present time. (1John 2:7)

Brethren, I write no new commandment unto you, but an old commandment which ye had from the beginning. The old commandment is the word which ye have heard from the beginning. Again, a new commandment, I write unto you, which thing is true in him and in you: because the darkness is past, and the true light now shineth." The former things are the former ways and teachings of Christ and the Apostles. (Isaiah 43:9) " Let all the nations be gathered together, and let the people be assembled; who among them can declare this, and show us former things?"

Knowledge of man will increase and advance. This knowledge is presently manifested by the development in technology and discovery made by science. Man will travel to and fro by means of speedy motor vehicles and flying machines. (Daniel 12:4) " But thou, O Daniel, shut up the words, and seal the book, and even to the time of the end: many shall run to and fro, and knowledge shall be increased." The Gospel of Christ will be preached all over the world. This is very obvious since there are many Christian converts now who have been studying and listening to the preaching of the Word. These are just some of the signs that we may notice happening in this present dispensation that will come to fulfill the prophecies in the bible. Thus, the coming of Christ is preceded by the signs stated in *Matthew 24:3-28.*

The Great Tribulation and the Catching Up in the Air

The Great Tribulation is the grim and dark event in the history of mankind accompanied by extreme agony and mourning after the tribulation preceding the coming of Christ. When the great tribulation occurs mankind shall be in great sorrow and distress, however, this will not be so long but because of the elect (chosen people of God) the agony will be shortened, thus, it will immediately commences the coming of Christ in the cloud.

This event has never happened before since the dawn of civilization and accordingly it will never happen again. The bible reveals an event of agony and extreme sorrow of the early Israelites that they were forced to kill and ate the flesh of their dead ones; but the great tribulation will be far more than this event because this has never come to the wild imagination of any man. What could this event be ?

When the entire earth is engulfed by chaos, panic, confusion agony, destruction, natural calamities such as volcanic eruption, earthquakes, floods, famine; pestilences; havocs and indescribable catastrophe everywhere and all forms of lawlessness where no man could ran away, clans of man will mourn in agony and torment. The sun will be darkened, and the moon will not give its light then the signs of the coming of the Son of Man will be seen or witnessed by all men descending from heaven with His angels with the sound of trumpet, prior to the ongoing universal campaign or religious revolution against the faithful, which could be the final battle or war on earth, that town and the flocks would be besieged, and there will be atrocities, genocide, mass slaughter

The bible tells the grim reality of that day (*Matthew 24:3-8/ 21-22/34,36*), " *those which be in Judean flee into mountains, let him which is in the housetop not come down to take anything out of his house; neither which is in the field return back to take his clothes*". It would be very pathetic for a woman feeding for her child because they will suffer hardship on that day of desolation. (*Matthew*

24:15-28-31) To those who may be living and witness, that day and the aftermath of that event could be unimaginable, and indescribably gruesome that perhaps no man has never thought in his wildest mind it would happen, in relation to the fact stated in the bible. Except that day be shortened no flesh will be left alive.

And the sun will be darkened, and the Son of Man will descend from the clouds. This significant and spectacular event will be witnessed by mankind on earth as the lightning cometh out of the east, and shineth even unto the west; so shall also the coming of the Son of Man be *(Matthew 24:27-29*) While the said events are taking place, in *the twinkling of an eye the saved Christians will be changed; the corruptible body will be changed into incorruptible one; at the last trump; the dead in Christ shall be raised (1Cor 15:52), and they shall all meet the Lord in the air* .Therefore, we cannot say that "catching up" may take place at any indeterminable time or hour; because these events that are mentioned in the bible already determine when rapture will take place. " *Catching Up*" shall be preceded by those events mentioned after the great tribulation.

Take note of the difference between the present-day and during the time of Christ; many impostors will appear in the last days and will claim for themselves and to the people that they are the Sent, Deliverer and Christ. Would you believe that during the Roman occupation of Jerusalem at the time of Christ no one was afraid to be identified with Christ because the government was ordering He and his followers to be arrested and tried for treason and deception? Even friends, Christians and disciples were afraid during that time because of Christian persecution and feared to be known and identified as Christ's allies. Remember the time when Christ foretold that He was to be denied thrice by His disciple Peter when the cock crowed? Peter denied that he would not do it and yet the prophecy of Christ happened. But in these days many have appeared representing themselves to be Christ's messenger or the Christ themselves because there is freedom, gain and opportunities as there is no more law against religion. These impostors are taking advantage to deceive and prosper in their sacrilegious and blasphemous activities.

Since there are rampant preaching everywhere in the world, the bible has always warned us to keep away from false teachings and prophets because they will mislead and lead you to destruction. If you happen to be in the false religion or church you may abandon it as the bible instructs us to cleave to that which is true. Do not be led to an impostor as the bible says in *Matthew 24:5, " For many shall come in my name, saying, I am Christ; and shall deceive many" What shall happen before the coming of our Lord Jesus Christ ?* Before the return of our Lord Jesus Christ, the earth shall be in trouble. There shall be tribulations and signs that shall determine his coming.

Matthew 24:3-8 say," *And as he sat upon the Mount of Olives, the disciples came unto him privately, saying, Tell us, when shall these things be? And what shall be the sign of they coming, and of the end of the world? And Jesus answered and said unto them, Take heed that no man deceive you. For many shall come in my name, saying, I am Christ; and shall deceive many. And ye shall hear of wars and rumors of wars; see that ye be not troubled; for all these things must come to pass, but the end is not yet. For nation shall rise against nation, and kingdom against kingdom; and there shall be famines and pestilence, and earthquakes, in divers places. All these are the beginning of sorrows."* The signs of the end is foretold by our Lord Jesus Christ. As you may observe in our time, there are many gospel preachers who even claim that they are the Christ. There are wars in different parts of the world. There are natural calamities anywhere on earth, famine, earthquakes, volcanic eruption. But according to the verse this is not yet the end but only a beginning of sorrow.

Another testimony can be read in *Luke 21:10-11* which say, " *Then said he unto them, Nation shall rise against nation, and kingdom against kingdom; and great earthquakes shall be in divers places, and famines, and pestilences; and fearful sights and great signs shall there be from heaven." When the great tribulation comes, remember that the coming of Christ is at hand, that is when we see signs from heaven. People shall greatly suffer hardships and even the people of God will suffer and be killed. What are those signs from heaven that shall signify the coming.*

Let us read, Acts 2:20, " the sun shall be turned into darkness, and the moon into blood, before the great and notable day of the Lord come:" When our Savior and Lord Jesus Christ returns on earth there shall be catching in the air of those who will be saved, and that shall happen instantly. Let us read *I Thessalonians 4:17* which says, " *then we which are alive and remain shall be caught up together with them in the clouds, to meet the Lord in the air; and so shall we ever be with the Lord." The coming of the Son of God shall be seen by all men around the globe. Revelation 1:7-11, say," Behold, he cometh with clouds; and every eye shall see him, and they also which pierced him: and all kindreds of the earth shall wail because of him. Even so , Amen." Therefore, as the verse says in his coming mankind shall wail.* After that, Christ will reign for a thousand years. Let us read *Revelation 20:4,"*

And I saw thrones, and they sat upon them, and judgment was given unto them: and I saw the souls of them that were beheaded for the witness of Jesus, and for the word of God, and which had not worshipped the beast, neither his image, neither had received his mark upon their foreheads, or in their hands; and they lived and reigned with Christ a thousand years."

Prior to this event, the martyrs in Christ who were killed shall suffer to give up their faith. During the great tribulation, when life shall be very difficult, people shall be forced to worship the beast(apostasy) and shall be forced to accept the mark in their foreheads the mark of the beast; which is described by the gestures and making the signs of 3 scores of 6 by their fingers in their right hand but to those who shall bear until the end shall be with Christ.

But after a thousand years had expired Satan shall be loosed out to deceive the nations. And to those who will not repent but go wicked shall be destroyed in the last day. Let us read *Revelation 20: 7-9," And when the thousand years are expired, Satan shall be loosed out of his prison, and shall go out to deceive the nations which are in the four quarters of the earth, Gog and Magog, to gather them together to battle: the number of whom is at the sand of the sea. And they went up on the breadth of the earth; and compassed the camp of the saints about, and the beloved city; and fire came down from God, out of heaven, and devoured them."*

The Coming of the Messiah

The coming of the Messiah is prophesied with the signs in the skies with the moon be darkened and the sun will not give its light. However, prior to this Jesus warned that our hearts be overcharged with surfeiting, and drunkenness, and cares of this life. Be aware that when those days come we must all be watchful to what is happening around us. Notice the emergence of false prophets, preaching in many places asking alms and by whatever means they will show you signs and wonders to deceive everyone.

Natural disasters such as earthquakes that have been causing lives and properties in many places. Fires ravaging the vast forests in big countries, flooding in many places, drought, famine, rampant hunger, wars in conflicting nations, volcanic eruptions and pestilences. These are the signs of times that are apparently happening in this generation. As the bible teaches in Luke 21:34-36 " And take heed to yourselves, lest at any time your hearts be overcharged with surfeiting, and drunkenness, and cares of this life, and so that day come upon you unawares. Foe as a snare shall it come on all them that dwell on the face of the whole earth. Watch ye therefore, and pray always, that ye may be accounted worthy to escape all these things that shall come to pass, and to stand before the Son of man.

Prelude To The End of Time

We are living in a period of time that is of overwhelming interest to all. Political leaders and legislators, men and women who hold positions of trust and authority, thinking men and women of all classes have their attention focused upon the events taking place around us. People are watching the strained, restless relations that exist between countries. Thousands observe the intensity that is taking possession of every earthly element and they realize that something great and decisive is about to happen—it appears that the world is on the verge of its most tremendous crisis.

Even with all the signs that are taking place there are many people who scoff at the idea that this world will come to an end. The earth will not just end the way people and visionaries visualize it. They think that the world will end a sudden burst or a sudden explosion brought by the release of disastrous nuclear bombs of superpowers or sudden strike and engulfing of tsunami brought by sudden impact of asteroids from the outer space. If it happens suddenly then no human beings would be spared but all will perish. What will happen to the promise of the written word? Who and what will be saved in the day of catching up in the air then? Therefore, it is a wrong notion. Earth will not suffer its sudden death just like that. Those things might happen in different areas of the earth but not as a whole that no one would be saved.

We should realize that the prophecy of Jesus Christ must be fulfilled first; that many occurrences shall be witnessed and experienced by mankind. There will be catastrophes, calamity, hunger which are all man's tribulation and then the great tribulation then shall catching up in the air shall follow in those days. Prior to the great tribulation are the signs in the sky, sun will be darkened, moon shall turn to red, there will be earthquake all around the four corners of the earth. And yet, after the catching up in the air has taken place, those dead in Christ would be raised first, and the Son of God will reign on earth a thousand years to those who would be preached and saved for the last chance. Then after a thousand years have elapsed, the second resurrection of the dead will occur to join nations to face judgment.

All things existing on earth shall melt because of the extreme and intense heat, thus, it will eventually burn and disappear from existence.(2Peter 3:10 says, " But the day of the Lord will come as a thief in the night; in the which the heavens shall pass away with a great noise, and the elements shall melt with fervent heat, the earth also and the works that are therein shall be burned up.") Thus, there will be new heaven and new earth after the disappearance of heavens and destruction of earth from extreme heat.

CHAPTER 15

The Process Of Punishment For Mankind

And after a thousand years of Christ's reign on earth is over the second resurrection shall take place and then the judgment day follows. For it is appointed unto man to die once and after that the judgment. All of us will face the judgment seat of the Lord God. In Acts 17:31 "Because he hath appointed a day, in the which he will judge the world in righteousness by that man whom he hath ordained; whereof he hath given assurance unto all men, in that he hath raised him from the dead."During the judgment hour, all nations in the world will be gathered and shall separate them one from another.

Why separate? Because those good nations will be separated from the bad nations. Like a goat to be separated from the throng of sheep. Matthew 25:32 says, " and before him shall be gathered all nations: and he shall separate them one from another, as a shepherd divided his sheep on his right hand, and but the goats, on the left." Those that will be saved to go on his right hand while those which will not be on his left hand. Matthew 25:33, " Then shall the King say unto them on his right, Come, ye blessed of my Father inherit the kingdom prepared for you from the foundation of the world."

Now, if you realize that you belong to the wrong church which is not the church of God that is being referred to in the bible that preaches the genuine word of God, do not hesitate to abandon it because there is judgment to those who follow and continuously follow the teachings of the wrong church upon knowing what is true but refuse to do so. Certain verse in the bible attests to that fact, in Revelation 18:4, "

And I heard another voice from heaven, saying, Come out of her, my people, that ye be not partakers of her sins, and that ye receive not of her plagues." Apparently, if you belong to this church you also partake her sins, you also sin as they sin and you will partake the plagues or punishments that will be inflicted upon them. The command in the said verse is clear, come out of her, meaning leave that false church because you will be partakers of their sins and the punishment that is intended for her.

The Apostle Paul, for instance, was brought up in the religion of Judaism during the time of Christ. He was a bad man before his calling but when he was called to serve God. He realized that he was in the false religion and belief. Paul's experience was a process along the way to Damascus when he was blinded and the rest is history.

He became a Christian convert and served God. While you have realized the truth, beware of dogs who will be judged accordingly. They will lead you to the pit of destruction because of false Christian doctrine. When you have learned and realized the genuine teachings of Christ you should abandon the false church. They will be used by Satan (who acts as angel of light) to teach different doctrines that are far from Christian doctrine.

They are called dogs by the bible. Who are those dogs? Isaiah 56:11 says , " Yes, they are greedy dogs which can never have enough, and they are shepherds that cannot understand: they all look to their own way, every one for his gain, from his quarter."These dogs are the shepherds or church leaders who deceive and do not understand what they are teaching, remotely different from the doctrine of Christ taught in the Church of God. These shepherds are teaching for themselves and for financial gain. Micah 3:11," The heads thereof judge for reward, and the priests thereof teach for hire, and the prophets thereof divine for money." There are many self-professed Christian churches which have different doctrines. We may not know the real motive for putting up their own church.

You may apparently notice that there are different titles and names of their churches which are not in the bible. But what the bible teaches about the true church of God is the Church of God . Let us read 2Corinthians 1:1 " Paul, an apostle of Jesus Christ by the will of God, and Timothy our brother, unto church of God which is at Corinth, with all the saints which are in all Achaia." There is only one true and genuine church that the bible is teaching other than that is false because false prophets and teachers obviously establish their own church. Romans 10:3 says, "

For they, being ignorant of God's righteousness, and going about to establish their own righteousness, have not submitted themselves unto the righteousness of God." They have not known the genuine teachings and instructions of the bible and they have not found it (Jeremiah 16:16) Their motive is for their gain (financial or quarter). Those false prophets, and self-proclaimed Christians but evil doers and workers shall be punished for they have commercialized the teachings of the Word and the motive is purely to gain from teaching and preaching. 2 Corinthians 2:17 says , " For we are not as many, which corrupt the word of God: but as of sincerity, but as of God in the sight of God speak we in Christ." They will face judgment for their inequities.

Those whose works are abominable in God's sight will be punished and they are those who are already segregated and out of the flock of God. Revelation 22:15, " For without are dogs, and sorcerers, and whoremongers, and murderers, and idolaters, and whosoever loveth and maketh a lie."

You may notice that there is an apparent strictness and inhibitions in many things because Christians or believers are taught discipline. But this discipline breeds love, joy, peace, and many good qualities for being children of God. They are called fruits of the spirit. Galatians 5:22, says " But the fruit of the Spirit is love, joy, peace, long-suffering, gentleness, goodness, faith, meekness, temperance; against such there is no law."

The path to salvation is narrow and not that wide as in those false churches whose paths are wide enough for them to perish. The second death is real. It is the punishment for people who are coward and unbelieving to the truth together with the evildoers. Revelation

21:8 says, " But the fearful, and unbelieving, and the abominable, and murderers, and whoremongers, and sorcerers, and idolaters, and all liars, shall have their part in the lake which burneth with fire and brimstone; which is the second death ." During the judgment day, nothing will be hidden but all man's secrets shall be exposed to be judged and punished. The hidden things of men shall come to be judged according to Ecclesiastes 12:14 saying, "For God shall bring every work into judgment, with every secret thing, whether it be good, or whether it be evil." Therefore, there is nothing to be hidden on that day. The secrets that men hid on earth shall all be exposed. Thus, the guilty ones shall be put to shame in this exposition of all the truths.

Evil men and evil doers will not escape that event t, and even the good deeds of men shall be receive their reward on that time. Another verse in Romans 2:16,says " in the day when God shall judge the secrets of men by Jesus Christ according to my gospel." While many sins are punishable , the time immemorial sin of idolatry is still a persisting sin of mankind up to the present time . The bible is warning us the punishment for this sin especially to those who have heard about the truth of the gospel but ignored it and keep heeding to the belief of idolatry shall be punished.

(Revelation 21:8) Their destiny is apparently hell and the wrath of God will be poured upon them. Revelation 14: 9-11, " and the third angel followed them, saying with a loud voice. If any man worship the beast and his image, and receive his mark in his forehead, or in his hand, the same shall drink of the wine of the wrath of God, which is poured out without mixture into the cup of his indignation, and he shall be tormented with fire and brimstone in the presence of the holy angels, and in the presence of the Lamb"

What is awful and excruciating is the pain of punishment to those who will not be saved but rather be thrown to fire. They will really feel the excruciating pain of fire but will remain alive during the torment because their bodies are in the flesh and blood as if they were on earth in the physical and human form. Many thought that in the day of punishment and judgment the physical bodies of the saved and the unsaved souls will both be transformed into different ones that are appropriate to their destination. Yes, correct. We will all be transformed into glorified bodies that is spirit because no flesh and blood shall enter heaven.

Those (the corporeal bodies) who will be saved and shall be raised from the dead in the coming of our Lord Jesus Christ shall be changed into incorruptible (heavenly) bodies, as what the bible tells in 1 Corinthians 15:53," For this corruptible must put on incorruption, and this mortal must put on immortality." This transformation will be appropriate only to those who will be saved. Their bodies will be changed into heavenly bodies because no flesh and blood and things that are corruptible can never enter the kingdom of God. But the unsaved cannot enter heaven but to eternal punishment. They will be given flesh and bones in order to face their punishment.

You may ask why do they not receive body that is appropriate in hell ? Into what body shall they be transformed? The one that is appropriate in hell? The punishment is in vain, therefore, if they will not feel the pain. There is no body form that will shield them and protect them from the excruciating pain of fire nor they will be given suits to ease the pain of punishment. That is why the smoke of torment will ascend.

The condemned will be literally in the flesh and blood when they will plunge the lake of burning sulfur. It constitutes practically, the sufferings of the unsaved ones. They will be tormented forever as the bible says, in Revelation 14: 11," and the smoke of their torment ascendeth up forever and ever, and they have no rest day nor night, who worship the beast and his image, and whosoever receiveth the mark of his name."

The sin of idolatry is a grave sin. There are many times in the bible that sin of idolatry is emphasized to be abominable in the sight of God and yet, many people who continuously follow this same belief seem to ignore this truth. But what is appalling is that those priests, and church leaders are not moved by the rebuke of the bible and yet they seemingly give no attention nor imperative action because they are bound by their church established doctrine .

But what is more appalling is that those traditional believers of the said faith may even reason out that they were born that way, they would die in the faith they were born, even if they know the truth perhaps because they are afraid of being persecuted. Deuteronomy 5:8 says, " Thou shalt not make thee any graven image, or any likeness of anything that is in heaven above, or that is in the earth beneath, or that is in the waters beneath the earth, thou shalt not bow down thyself unto them, nor serve them,"

Whatever happens during the hour of judgment God will be the sole judge. We cannot judge those people now because salvation is God's. God will have mercy to those whom He wants to give mercy. God knows the truth and searches the hearts of men.

Customs & Tradition that men consider in their worship of their gods have become a burden and obstacles for them to accept the truth of the gospel. Men may enjoy the comfort and happiness of customs and tradition and may even believe that it can save and make them good but they do not realize that such a thing is nothing. It may lead them to punishment or eternal torment and they do not know that what they are doing is abominable in the sight of the living God. Jeremiah 10:3-5 say, " For the customs of the people are vain: for one cutteth a tree out of the forest, the work of the hands of the workman, with the axe.

They deck it with silver and with gold; they fasten it with nails and with hammers, that it move not." As you can read in these verses which are being referred to an idol in which men make by means of wood, they deck it with silver and gold, as they fasten it with nails and hammers in order that it shall not move. In other words, it's a useless object that men do. Habakkuk 2:18-19 say, " What profiteth the graven image that the maker thereof hath graven it; the molten image, and a teacher of lies, that the maker of his work trusteth therein, to make dumb idols. Woe unto him that saith in the wood, Awake; to the dumb stone, Arise, it shall teach! Behold, it is laid over with gold and silver, and there is no breath at all in the midst of it."

Apparently, this graven image that is made by the hands of men is useless and dumb and should not be bowed down. You can just imagine, you, who are not aware of the danger of this faith, all your life worship, pray and even walk a procession for the piece of wood and stone that mean nothing but abomination in the sight of God, the real Creator, who is worthy of praise and worship. Remember, God is a spirit and all who believe in Him must worship in Spirit and Truth. This is a very clear instruction of the gospel. This pronouncement is proven and affirmed in John 4:24, " God is a Spirit; and they that worship him must worship him in spirit and in truth."

The Judgment of the Living and the Dead

The living who were caught up in the air shall be with the Lord and the dead in Christ shall be risen first in the judgment day. Let us read I Corinthians 15:51-52," Behold, I show you a mystery; We shall not all sleep, but we shall all be changed, In a moment, in the twinkling of an eye, at the last trump; for the trumpet shall sound, and the dead shall be raised incorruptible, and we shall be changed.

For this corruptible must put on incorruption, and this mortal must put on immortality. So when this corruptible shall have put on incorruption, and this mortal shall have put on immortality, then shall be brought to pass the saying that is written, Death is swallowed up in victory." Therefore, those who shall be saved shall be changed at the twinkling of an eye because their bodies which are flesh and blood cannot enter the kingdom of heaven but they have to be changed to incorruptible bodies. And the dead in Christ shall be risen first, then finally those who were bound to hell will also be risen to face judgment.

They will rise from the grave to receive physical bodies. Let us read Ezekiel 37:5-7," Thus saith the Lord GOD unto these bones; Behold, I will cause breath to enter into you, and ye shall live: and I will lay sinews upon you, and will bring up flesh upon you, and cover you with skin, and put breath in you, and ye shall live; and ye shall know that I am the LORD."Therefore, the bones in the grave shall be covered again with flesh, with skin, and will receive again breath of life to know the Lord GOD. Those who will be bound to hell shall remain in the state with flesh and bone, so that by the time they are cast to hell they shall really feel the excruciating and tormenting pain of punishment in the lake of burning sulfur.

The Tormenting Lake of Fire

Who will experience the tormenting pain in hell? We should not accuse nor condemn anybody of his guilt nor judge anyone by what he did because we are not to judge men but only God. In the day of judgment, the bible reveals, that there are those who will be punished for their wickedry and infirmity. Let us read John 12:48 which says," He that rejecteth me, and receiveth not my words, hath one that judgeth him; the word that I have spoken, the same shall judge him in the last day."

Therefore, Christ said, those who refuse to receive his teachings or words shall be judged by the Word according to the bible. Another sector who will be judged according to their ways can be read in 2Corinthians 2:17," For we are not as many, which corrupt the word of God: but as of sincerity, but as of God, in the sight of God speak we in Christ." These are the false prophets who deceive people by teaching the word in a wrong motive but for financial gains and self-interest. Those self-confessed and false prophets and teachers who for their vile motives would say on that day that they have healed the sick and driven out devils in His name.

Let us read Matthew 25:41," Then shall he say also unto them on the left hand, Depart from me, ye cursed, into everlasting fire, prepared for the devil and his angels;" Literally, they are false prophets who are out of this world deceiving many to damnation. The bible is warning us about these agents of the devil. Let us read Isaiah 56:11" Yes, they are greedy dogs which can never have enough, and they are shepherds that cannot understand; they all look from his quarter." Expressly, when these shepherds ask too much of you, then they are the ones being referred to as greedy dogs.

The bible also tells us those beast or the devil worshippers will be punished. Let us read Revelation 13:4," And they worshiped the dragon which gave power unto the beast; and they worshipped the beast, saying, Who is like unto the beast? Who is able to make war with him?" The dragon or the beast being referred here is Satan and his cohorts who will be thrown into hell. Revelation 12:9," And the great dragon was cast out, that old serpent, called the Devil, and Satan, which deceiveth the whole world: he was cast out into the earth, and his angels were cast out with him." The same fate will happen to those who worship idols, liars and others being mentioned..

Let us read, Revelation 21:8," But the fearful, and unbelieving, and the abominable, and murderers, and all liars, shall have their part in the lake which burneth with fire and brimstone: which is the second death."Those enumerated in the bible shall also be punished such as these in I Corinthians 6:9-10." Know ye not that the unrighteous shall not inherit the kingdom of God? Be not deceived: neither fornicators, nor idolaters, nor adulterers, nor effeminate, nor abusers of themselves with mankind, nor thieves, nor covetous, nor drunkards, nor revilers, nor extortioners, shall inherit the kingdom of God."

Abominable works of any person are absolutely punishable like this one mentioned in Deuteronomy 18:10-13 " There shall not be found among you any one that maketh his son or his daughter to pass through the fire, or that useth divination, or an observer of times, or an enchanter, or a witch, or a charmer, or a consulter with familiar spirits, or a wizard, or a necromancer, For all that do these things are an abomination unto the LORD; and because of these abominations the LORD thy God doth drive them out from before thee."

Idolatry and Its Punishment

Many times in the bible did idolatry was mentioned as abomination in the sight of the Lord. Even in the olden times idolatry was an abominable act of men and commanded by God to discard and prohibited to do. The LORD God commanded the first people of Israel not to bow down before any graven images. In Deuteronomy 5: " thou shalt not bow down thyself unto them, nor serve the for I the LORD thy God am a jealous God, visiting, the iniquity of the father upon the children unto the third and fourth generation of them that hate me."

In this present Christian dispensation many idolaters have been persisting their idolatrous activities in many occasions and yet they are not aware of the coming punishment to them that violate the LORD's commandment on idolatry. As they are continuously idolatrous in many ways they are also blasphemers that they even use the name of the LORD in vain.

They even changed the name of the Lord as they utter the word without hesitation into, "Bro" or sometimes, "Papa" and other names of their own. This is a clear blasphemy and a violation of the God's commandment which states that you should not use the name of the Lord thy God in vain. These people are without respect and totally blinded by the god of this world as they worship idols and perform senseless rituals that have nothing to do with their salvation. In fact, the bible attests against the idolaters who have changed the truth of God into a lie.

Romans 1:25 says, " who changed the truth of God into a lie, and worshipped and served the creature more than the Creator, who is blessed forever. Amen." The bible says that their gods cannot speak because they are only part of the tree and a mere wood. Jeremiah 10:5 says, " They are upright as the palm tree, but speak not; they muse needs be borne, because they cannot go. Be not afraid of them; for they cannot do evil, neither also is it – in them to do good." Habakkuk 2:18-19 say, What profiteth the graven image that the maker thereof hath graven it; the molten image, and a teacher of lies, that the maker of his work trusteth therein, to make dumb idols? Woe unto him that saith to the wood, Awake! Behold, it is laid over with gold and silver, and there is no breath at all in the midst of it."

The said verses will prove that the god of the idolaters are nothing but a mute and dumb piece of wood while they even melt and mold them with gold and silver and yet no breath in it. What happens to this idol worshippers in the last day or in judgment day? Revelations 21: says, " But the fearful, and unbelieving, and the abominable, and murderers, and whoremongers, and sorcerers, and idolaters, and all liars, shall have their part on the lake which burneth with fire and brimstone which is the second death."

The Taste of Heaven and Hell

How does it feel being in heaven on that day? This is what the holy people or the saved ones going to experience in heaven: Revelation 21:4, " And God shall wipe away all tears from their eyes; and there shall be no more death, neither sorrow, nor crying, neither shall there be any more pain: for the former things are passed away." The saved ones will receive a white stone for their new names.

Let us read, Revelation 2:17." He that hath an ear, let him hear what the Spirit saith unto the churches; To him that overcometh will I give to eat of the hidden manna, and will give him a white stone, and in the stone, a new name written, which no man knoweth saving he that receiveth it." There will be joyous singing of the angels and saints in Revelation 5:9" And they sung a new song, saying, Thou art worthy to take the book, and to open the seals thereof;"

How does it feel being in hell on that day? As mentioned earlier those evildoers; Satan and his angels will be thrown in the lake of fire. Revelation 14:9-11 say, " And the third angel followed them, saying with a loud voice, If any man worship the beast and his image, and receive his mark in his forehead, or in his hand, the same shall drink of the wine of the wrath of God, which is poured out without mixture into the cup of his indignation; and he shall be tormented with fire and brimstone in the presence of the holy angels, and in the presence of the Lamb' and the smoke of their torment ascendeth up forever and ever; and they have no rest day nor night, who worship the beast and his image, and whosoever receiveth the mark of his name."

As mentioned earlier those human beings who would be punished would be in the state of human flesh and blood that they might really feel the torment of hell. In heaven, after the triumph of the overcomers, there will no more day and night, no more Sabbath, no more hunger, tears, hardships nor sufferings, no more things of the past. These are all asserted in Revelation 7:15-16, Revelation 21:24.

CHAPTER 16

Religion In American History

American Separatism from the Secular World

In many nations religion plays an important role in man's endeavor . Religious color surfaces in all man's struggle in order to live with freedom and independence from others' interference, persecution and dominance. The birth and conquest of a nation was associated with religious color and politics as well and which served as factors to isolate a minority group from the overwhelming majority.

The birth of America that was called by the early European settlers as the New World passed through the bloody process before it was won. It was a long process whose root cause from the mother land, England was religion in nature. England was formerly a Roman Britain which eventually released its dominance to the land because of the growing protest of the protestants in Europe. They did not want the Roman Catholic faith and belief for it was far beyond the way the Christian church in the Church of England worshipped God.

Feeling uncomfortable as the atmosphere of persecution pervaded the Englishmen they left the land to sail to the New World in the hope to find their place. They called themselves Puritans from the word "pure". The Puritans were not the first inhabitants in the land of the native Indians but there existed the original inhabitants called the red Indians.

Columbus called them Indians thinking that he had just discovered islands between China and India. The people in America had resemblance and physical appearance that of Indians in the India that he mistakably called them Indians. The name Indians eventually spread to the people and explorers who went there.

However, there were already many foreigners from other lands that went to Americas particularly from Europe. The Englishmen had to ask permission from the king of England before they had to go to America which was their colony during that time. It was the age of numerous explorations in many parts of the world. European explorers were most popular and rivaling in the conquest of other land around the globe.

The story of the Puritans and Separatists was an ecstacy and agony for most religious people who wanted to find a place for their beliefs to be most suited. The birth of the New World was started by the Puritans in search for liberty to live and worship God.

The Puritans Sail to the New World

In 1620, the pilgrims disembarked on the seashores of Plymouth, Massachusetts in Northern American. The historic migration of the pilgrims from the Old World(England) marked a saga of a new beginning in the so-called New World (America).

Today, that memorable arrival of the American forefathers in the American soil was engraved in the gigantic granite-stone tablet known as the Plymouth Rock, four hundred years ago . Many know the adventurous journey of the first Pilgrims from Old England embarked the ship named Mayflower. Subsequently, their long journey from England to America started the establishment of the first US colonies.

Who were the so-called Pilgrims? Why did they quest for new settlement in the American land? Was religion the main reason why they left England?

Turbulent Times for Religious People in England

A hundred years before the pilgrims left England, the Roman Catholic England was under the kingship of King Henry VIII, who had the title of the "Protector of the Believers" bestowed upon him by Pope. However, a feud between Pope Clement VII and King

Henry began when the Pope refused to nullify the marriage of Henry and Catherine of Aragon, the first of the six wives of the king.

At that time the Roman Catholic church was having a hard time with the growing population of protestant-reformists in large part of Europe while King Henry was muddling with his family problems. Henry did not allow the influence of the reformists inside England for fear of losing the honor and title given to him by the Roman Catholic church.

But eventually, he changed his mind because of the church's refusal to annul his marriage with Catherine of Aragon, thereby, negating the power and influence of the Catholic church in England. In 1534, King Henry pronounced his final decision of nixing the control of the Pope over the Catholics in England and declared himself as the supreme ruler of the Church of England.

In the meantime, he ordered the closure of the monasteries and auctioned some the big properties of the catholic church. Eventually, England became a protestant country when King Henry died in 1547. After his death Edward VI who succeeded his throne did not submit to the religious authority of the Pope, and after Edward's death in 1553, Mary, a catholic daughter of King Henry to Catherine of Aragon, became the Queen of England attempted to betray the nation under the authority of the Pope.

She coercively ordered the deportation of many protestants and burned alive more than 300 of them by the court of Inquisition. Inquisition was a form of court trial which imposed penalty to heretics. Heretics were those belligerent people who were convicted as enemies of the ruling authority, that is why Mary was given the name of Bloody Mary of England.

However, the reformists could not stop to employ the much-needed reforms . Mary died in 1558, after which her step sister, Elizabeth I succeeded her in power and gave the nation an assurance of an absolute freedom from the Pope's influence and obliteration of the religious influence in the lives of the English people. Likewise, the separation of the Roman Catholic church from England was not that easy.

The protestants had to remove absolutely any mark of influence in their lives, and if possible, even to the memory of every citizen about the church. The protestants wanted to refine their way of living particularly their religious beliefs and manner of worshipping God, that is why they were called Puritans (from the word "pure"). To the Puritans, they needed not any Pope nor bishop to influence their belief in God, and eventually pronounced that the church congregation and its affairs separate from the affairs of the state. They were later called, "Separatists".

During the time of Elizabeth I, puritan-critics emerged to criticized the system of non-formal adherence to the norms of the decree being complied by the nation. The Queen did not like the manner of non-formal attire of the clergies and ordered the Archbishop of Canterbury in 1564 to enforce a law and issue a decree concerning proper attire or implementing a dress code.

The Puritans felt and foresaw the restoration of the same dress code of the Catholic priests, they opposed and disobeyed the decree of the Queen. There were subsequent turbulent events in the church history in England during the emergence of hierarchical priesthood which Elizabeth asked an assurance from the bishops and priests by compulsory ordering them to take an oath of allegiance and loyalty, in which she was the supreme ruler of the church.

Pilgrims' Conversion to Separatism

When Elizabeth died, she was succeeded to the throne in 1603 by James I, who severely persecuted the Separatists, so that by force they would learn to obey his authority. In 1608, a group of separatists left clandestine departure, the town of Scooby to migrate to Holland to find freedom.

Consequently, after some time they felt the atmosphere of discomfort by the apparent low morale of the people from different religious groups which according to them were consented by the Dutch authority. Later on they decided to finally abandoned Europe and found their way to North American where they settled for good. The separatists were apparently prepared for a lengthy voyage just to find settlement and freedom for their belief and in the passage of time their long journey they were called the Pilgrims.

The pilgrims sought permission from the King of England that they would settle with many separatists who joined them in Virginia, a colony of Britain on September, 1620 on board the ship Mayflower. A group of almost a hundred adult pilgrims and youths persevered the inclement weather in the midst of the stormy journey for about two months in the Atlantic Ocean before finally reaching their destination in Cape Cod in West Virginia.

It was a hundred miles away from their country of origin. At that point, in Mayflower they wrote a pact known as the "Pact of Mayflower" which stated their general intention of creating a community and making this decree their law to be obeyed by all. They settled near Plymouth on December 21, 1620.

New Beginning in the New World

After a few months, many of the puritans died due to unbearable climate change and severe cold that brought them illnesses and those who were physically weak succumbed to death. After the passage of the winter season, they were so delighted by the spring season when they found time to build shelter for their comfort as they learned to grow crops from the native American Indians. When autumn came in 1621, they saw the fruit of their toil by the progress and prosperity of their community as they found it necessary to set a day for thanksgiving to the Lord God for the blessings they had received despite the hardship they suffered through the years.

In this occasion, the feast of thanksgiving, since then, became an annual celebration until the present time in the United States and other parts of the world having the same belief. Many foreigners arrived in the colony in Plymouth. What matters most was the rapid growth of population within fifteen (15) years time which exceeded to more than 2,000 people. Meanwhile, other puritans in England believed that the promise land for them, Separatists, was just located across the other side of the Atlantic ocean. In 1630, one of their groups went to the Northern part of Plymouth, and established the Massachusetts Bay Colony. In 1640, more than 20,000 English settlers lived in New England.

When Massachusetts Bay Colony controlled Plymouth in 1691. The pilgrims -separatists converged in Boston to be the center of their religious worship in the colony. The separatists joined the puritans who were the authority for religious beliefs in New England.

The Puritans' fashion of Worshipping God

The puritans in the New World established and built first their worship center made of wood where they would assemble to worship God every Sunday morning. The worshippers would painstakingly bear the condition inside the worship house when the weather was fine, but their worship service may or may not be able to bear the extreme cold during winter while their faith was tested in the same situation for most devoted puritans.

At the time there was no heating system yet that would keep them warm inside their wooden house, that is why they couldn't bear the frost biting cold which oftentimes downed the weak and unstable-bodied worshippers. The preachers wore gloves during the church service as they texted the religious messages with the accompaniment of their hands giving emphasis on the importance of the messages.

The Puritans patterned their religious teachings from the fashion of the French-Protestants particularly from the teaching-advocacy of John Calvin.. They believed that God had destined their fate and whatever happened to them was God's will for them.

Accordingly, It was also God who judge mankind, saved the deserving people and punished those who became disobedient to his commandments. Their religious doctrine stated that a dead man did not know if he would be able to escape the fiery lake of fire or would see the glory of heavens. The Puritan-teachers taught also repentance among the sinners, that they would go to hell if they would disobey God's laws, and the more they would emphasize man's penitence in order to be saved, to be more obedient to the doctrines of the church.

The early puritan faith teachers would often times emphasized or highlighted the importance of repentance and salvation. One teacher by the name of Jonathan Edwards preached in the congregation the critical issue entitled, "The Sinners in the Hands of the Wrath of God". He portrayed the terrible sufferings of those; who would not be saved in the last days as horrible an unimaginable and dreadful as the listeners were scared and worried for their souls in the life after death.

The safety of the evangelists who preached with scary tales that usually scared and alarmed the worshippers were endangered and got banned to preach in Massachusetts. The authority expelled one preacher named, Mary Dyer, three times but in many occasions was able to return and preach the same messages. Consequently, they caught her and sentenced her to death in Boston on July 1, 1660. The attitude of the religious leaders of the puritans as so harsh when it comes to profession religious faith that was not in conformity with their religious doctrines in which Philip Ratcliffe, a preacher who had forgotten the do's and don'ts in the colony.

Unfortunately, they captured Ratcliffe in one of his speech engagements in Salem and was ordered a penalty of public whipping and had his ears cut before he was freed, in order that he might able to remember the laws of the land. Because of the extreme restrictions and harsh laws of the puritans, many people left Massachusetts as they deployed to other American colonies.

Violence in the Colony and the Failures of the Puritans

While the puritans believed and treated themselves as God's chosen people, they became arrogant and conceited as they mistreated others particularly the native American Indians as the lower grade type of human species and looked down to them as filthy people and squatters in the land. Because of this undesirable and grave misconduct of the puritans towards the native American Indians, the sentiment of the latter led them to become hostile and vindictive against the puritans. The rebellious native Indians attacked the puritan settlers.

They never thought that the outcome of their vanity would lead to violence and eventually the puritan leaders became lenient and gradually lifted the harsh laws they enforced in the colony to avoid violence. They amended the same laws about the Sabbath in order to allow members to carry protective firearms on their way to worship house. In 1675 the situation worsened, when King Philip or otherwise known as Metacomet of Wampanoag American Indians attacked the puritans for fear of losing some territories for his fellow-American Indians. The Indians burned their houses, massacred the settlers and in retaliation, the puritans vindictively fought back in subsequent battles which lasted for a number of months.

In 1676, Philip was captured in Rhode Island and he was terribly beheaded while his body was cut into four(4) pieces, which eventually ended the war with the puritans. The native Indians submitted to the authority in later years. In 18th century, the puritans declared their enthusiasm in methodologies. They criticized some church ministers in Massachusetts in their leadership in England and intensified their desire for liberty. They associated religion with politics in solving national problems. The puritans were known to be religious devotees, enthusiastic and brave when it come to the issue of religion. It was a word of mouth that they were loyal people.

To sum up the whole story, the Puritans left England because of religious persecution, and they wanted to look a place where they can conduct pure worship of God. However, when they went to Holland they were not persecuted there because Holland was a country open to all kinds of religion. They left Holland for New World because the Pilgrims did not want to grow their children in a Dutch upbringing or their children may no longer speak their language.

Was it justifiable to cleanse people's heart by coercing them to obey with they did not believe in?

Was it justifiable to associate religion with politics in order solve national issues and problems?

Was there a need to separate the church from the state? What were the implications?

Nowadays, in many countries, Is there a separation of church and state?

Early Explorers – Were they Christians? What were their objectives in the Colonization? During the age of explorations and discoveries many explorers were Europeans. Many of them went their ways to different parts and ends of the globe in search for wealth, trade, goods, colonies and many more. One of the most famous European explorers was the Portuguese (naturalized Spanish) navigator and discoverer of the Philippine archipelago was Ferdinand Magellan.

The Author

Artusard Renault – is an author, spiritualist, lecturer or teacher, researcher and a Barrister who writes academic books, history, religion and spiritual issues for learning. His surname bears the famous Parisian brand Renault, but did not claim that he is secretively related to the iconic French business tycoon .However, the said author's name has a long story to tell but not in this point in time. He is a member of the *Church of God International.* His book about *Codex Sinaiticus* is a significant and substantial writings of revelation that he believes no religious and spiritual teacher -writers can parallel and substantiate the emptiness of other Christian denominations to understand in a significant manner as he believes that such teachings can only be available at the *Church of God*. The renown name is a pen name of *Bro. Artemio Saguinsin*.

BIBLIOGRAPHY

The King James version of the Bible

The Teachings of the Messenger Of God in the last days

About the Author

The author is a book author-writer, researcher, lecturer-teacher, religion and spiritual enthusiast. He has been publishing a lot of titles about his profession in business and law. Hence, a number of religion books for guidance and education for populace from various denominations.

Read more at https://tinyurl.com/arenault.

About the Publisher

www.ingramcontent.com/pod-product-compliance
Lightning Source LLC
LaVergne TN
LVHW090357210926
848480LV00002B/370
9798231867998